To|
Glok

Stev

A PERSONAL
BRAND
STORY

From the Author of Amazon No.1 Global sensation
"Top Biller – The Life of a Recruiter"

Printed in the United Kingdom
First Printing, 2021

ISBN: 978-1-9162459-2-1 (Paperback)
ISBN: 978-1-9162459-3-8 (eBook)

SGuest Publishing
Walsall, WS9 0DN

steve@sguest.co.uk

Contents

ACKNOWLEDGEMENTS   7

FOREWORD   9

ABOUT THE AUTHOR   11

INTRODUCTION   13
Why did I write this book?
Why do I think that building a personal brand is important?   14
'Youngling Steve', the kid who shaped my personal brand.   15

CHAPTER 1: WHAT MAKES YOU DIFFERENT?   21

CHAPTER 2: WHAT IS A PERSONAL BRAND
AND WHY IS IT IMPORTANT?   27
The 2018 whirlwind   28
What is a personal brand?   32
What does an effective personal brand do?   35

CHAPTER 3: THE BOOK – MY TOP BILLER –
'THE LIFE OF A RECRUITER' STORY   37
Writing your own book   40
Exposure   45
How I published the book   46
How to get ideas   47

CHAPTER 4: THE POWER YOUR PERSONAL BRAND HOLDS   49

Consistency   51

Defining the brand   54

Give more than you take   56

Stay humble   57

CHAPTER 5: SOCIAL MEDIA – THE POWER OF CONSISTENCY   61

How to get started with social media   62

The 70/20/10 split   63

Internationally/nationally trending posts   64

Victories and wins   66

Business and industry trends   66

Positive quotes   67

Engaging content   68

Don't pitch, define   69

The Business Development Challenge   75

CHAPTER 6: HOW TO GROW YOUR NETWORK   79

Helping others to help you   80

Who stays and who goes?   82

Buying followers – yes or no?   83

Influential people   84

Podcasts and interviews   84

Keep ahead of the curve   85

CHAPTER 7: ADDING VALUE   89

Following my journey   90

Ways I have added value in the last twelve months.   91

Collaboration within competition   95

CHAPTER 8: JOURNALING   97

CHAPTER 9: YOUR NETWORK IS YOUR NETWORTH   131

Building a reputation using your network   132

Gaining perspective from your network   134

CHAPTER 10: LEVERAGE 137

Implementation 139

The importance of having a mentor or coach 140

CHAPTER 11: DIFFERENTIATE YOURSELF 143

You can add value 144

Be ahead of the curve 148

Differentiation is a mindset shift 149

CHAPTER 12: THE HATERS 151

CONCLUSION 159

A personal brand journey summary 161

Acknowledgements

I never imagined that I would write a book, let alone write two books.

I have surrounded myself with professionals. Thank you again to my Editor in Chief, Ms. Claire Robbin, for waving a magic wand over my scrawl and making it readable and engaging. Thanks also to the exceptionally well managed Sam Pearce of SWATT Books. She has again made bringing a book to publication effortless and fun.

A huge thank you must go to every person that bought a copy of my first book, 'Top Biller – The Life of a Recruiter'. The overwhelming belief in the book's concept and the outpouring of kind words from readers gave me the impetus and motivation to write another book. Also, the support from my network, friends, colleagues, ex-colleagues, mentees, mentors and beyond has been incredible! I feel championed by you all, thank you.

Embarking on the writing of 'A Personal Brand Story' has highlighted the various influential people who have helped me along the journey. Whether it be the person who knocked on my university residence door or the business coaches who have guided me, I am thankful for everybody involved in my journey. I believe that it's crucial to consistently surround yourself with people who will allow you to reach your full potential, but even more importantly, to give credit where credit is due. The people that shape our lives are those we hold close, connect, and engage with, and we should acknowledge them whenever we can.

The biggest thank you is to my wife, Emma, who has supported me throughout, without question, doubt or judgement. Emma is amazing in every way and paves the way for me to continue on this journey. I will always be eternally grateful for the 'unseen' jobs she does in the background that allow me the opportunity to push forward, not to mention being a wonderful mum to our two beautiful boys, Ethan and Hugo.

I trust you will enjoy reading about my journey and find the content has value and pointers to implement into your own success story.

Good luck!

Foreword

There is one clear truth out there; the people that get personal branding right often achieve incredible success. I know it has opened many doors for me, and I am fortunate to know many others who have achieved so much by getting their personal brands right.

I met Steve digitally a couple of years ago after we both published our first books (Steve's first book "Top Biller" and my first book "The Million-Pound LinkedIn Message"). What stood out to me from the very first conversation we had was that Steve was determined, passionate and driven to help as many people as he could. What he has achieved over the last couple of years is the reason this book is so valuable and a must-read for anyone ready to start building their personal brand.

The term "Personal Brand" is thrown around a lot, mostly by people telling you how important it is, how EVERYONE needs to have a personal brand. As true as that may be, they rarely tell you how you can actually build one.

Well, here is the book we have been waiting for.

Steve Guest has built a hugely successful personal brand and has leveraged social media to achieve success in so many areas of his business. With this book he has done what very few do, he shows you how he did it, and how you can do it to.

Throughout the book Steve goes into real detail into his story, from before he embarked on his personal brand journey, to every step along the way. What I thought was a brilliant addition was the inclusion of his journey writing his first book "Top Biller". Writing a book isn't easy but can have a huge impact on your personal brand. Steve talks you through his writing and publishing journey which is powerful for anyone wanting to take their personal brand to that next level.

The standout part of this book for me is the focus around consistency. It is a crucial part of personal brand success on social media and Steve digs deep into it. He includes plans, ideas, challenges and more to help you get started and remain consistent. Pay attention to this chapter!

You'll also enjoy Steve sharing real segments from his social media journal which he kept during this personal branding journey. These unique insights add a human layer to the book, helping you as the reader connect even deeper to the process.

Here is my advice, read this once and consume the story. Then work through it again whilst putting together a game plan to launch YOUR personal brand. Listen to what Steve is advising you to do, apply his strategies, keep consistent and I have no doubt you'll be surprised at the impact it has on you, your business and your results.

Daniel Disney
Author of 'The Million-Pound LinkedIn Message'
& 'The Ultimate LinkedIn Sales Guide'

About the Author

Steve Guest is a degree educated, qualified buyer (MCIPS) & recruiter (MREC) and author of the book Amazon #1 Global Sensation 'Top Biller – Life of a Recruiter' which has sold in over 40 countries.

Born and bred in the West Midlands, Steve has specialised in building recruitment businesses, new regions and brands whilst empowering and mentoring recruitment consultants into achieving Top Biller status. Guest has operated within the recruitment industry for over 15 years, working for large globally recognised recruitment PLC brands to founding S Guest Consultancy Services Ltd. Guest is an expert at driving innovation and growth, both for individuals and the recruitment industry. As Founder and Mentor of the 12-Week Recruitment Mastery Programme, Guest is at the forefront of a new dawn for the recruitment industry, which aims to refresh the industry's reputation, and offer a platform and forum for recruiters to discuss pain points, successes, and add value as a united force.

Steve still actively recruits and continues to retain regional billing records for some of the biggest and well-known brands within the recruitment industry.

Steve is also a recognised public event and keynote speaker, presenter of 'The Guestlist Podcast with Steve Guest', which is listed in the global top 80 business podcasts, and founder and host of 'The Guestlist' YouTube channel.

Steve enjoys a number of sports including football, hockey and golf, and is husband to Emma, and proud Dad to Ethan and Hugo.

Introduction

"Your brand is your public identity, what you're trusted for. And for your brand to endure, it has to be tested, redefined, managed, and expanded as markets evolve. Brands either learn or disappear".

— Lisa Gansky

What is a personal brand, and how would you like to present your personal brand to the world? If you're not sure about the answers, you are in the right place.

This book follows my personal brand journey, and you are a welcome voyeur to all the good, the bad and the ugly of it. Welcome to 'The Steve Guest Brand'.

How my brand looks today is not how it looked in the beginning, but the principles have remained the same. Using my own journey as the roadmap, I want to show you how you too can begin your own personal brand. Most importantly, I would like to help you stay consistent in your personal branding efforts.

Why did I write this book? Why do I think that building a personal brand is important?

I didn't plan a personal brand journey, and in all honesty, I don't know where it is all heading. I never foresaw the amazing things that have happened so far, and I can't begin to imagine where it will take me next. I am certain, however, that a strong personal brand journey will positively impact you as an individual and the people around you. I was always aware that a solid personal brand would bring about extra opportunities, but I never could have predicted the diverse and exciting openings this journey has created for me.

In the beginning, in the day-to-day humdrum of the recruitment world, I was taught the following:

"Tell *everyone* what you do. Tell them what you specialise in and the difference you can make to them. The more people that know what you can do, the bigger your market potential. In return you will make more placements and experience more success."

This teaching made perfect sense to me; a strong personal brand could help me place more people, earn more money, and achieve greater success. Simple!

What I didn't understand or consider in the beginning was how a strong personal brand could create so many branches of opportunities with countless diverse outcomes.

Since I embarked on my personal brand journey, I have met incredible people and learnt from truly awe-inspiring leaders and mentors. These inspiring individuals have motivated me to share my journey, add value, create content and maintain strategically placed processes and procedures. The ability to consistently generate value with no expectation of return is a tough ask. Still, I believe the overall mission must be even more significant than what you believe you can change. You must attack it day by day, bit by bit; find where you can add value and keep showing up. In a nutshell, that's all I have done.

Be genuine, transparent, authentic, and set out your stall.

Undoubtedly, people will try and drag you down, and that's ok; it's part of the process, and you must try to embrace it. There will always be people who won't agree with you, like you, or appreciate your efforts. Many will happily inform you of such. It *will* happen, so don't be naïve, believing you are exempt – go in with your eyes wide open, learn, improve, implement and grow. That's all any of us can do.

At the beginning of your personal brand journey, you almost certainly won't achieve the next viral post; most likely, you won't get any interaction at all! That's fine; we've all been there. Remember, it's a journey and not a race to the finish line.

We get one shot at this life, so enjoy it, go with it and have fun!

I hope sharing my personal brand journey will motivate you to begin your own. It's worth it if you persevere.

'Youngling Steve', the kid who shaped my personal brand.

My work attitude, as with many people, was primarily formed during my school years. Whether this attitude is part of my nature or down to how my environment nurtured me, I don't fully know – all I do know is that I worked particularly hard at school and loved academia. I didn't possess an unusually high IQ, but I was consistently willing to put in the effort to become as good as I could be. Plus, I experienced enduring anxiety of never wanting to let anyone down. I desired to achieve good grades and make people happy, and if that meant putting in the extra effort and working to the highest standard, then that's what I did.

This attitude came at a high cost, however. As I grew up and matured, I continued to be the student that raced to catch the early bus home to get my homework done promptly. I was diligent – I was never late, I treated everyone and *everything* with respect and was rarely in trouble. No prizes for guessing that I didn't quite make it to the 'cool' gang, but I was never an outsider either. I sat somewhere in-between, accepted by the cool gang but not invited. It so happened that I looked after the kids that got bullied and was not shy about standing up for injustice in the playground.

This attitude ultimately meant that academia and schoolwork came first. The 'usual' teen years of social bonding, like going to the pub, late-night drinking, and meetups in the park were not in my modus operandi. Unlike most lads my age, my first pint in a pub was with my Dad – bless him. To this day, the memory of that first pint means the world to me.

As I was coming to the end of my schooling, I was still somewhat naïve, unassuming, and lacking confidence and self-belief. I thus decided to go to university to both further my academics and find some self-reliance. I wanted to study Graphic Design at university, as this was an area that I was keen to explore. But, me being me, logic took over, and I ended up signing up for a BSc in Accounting & Finance and Marketing Management. This choice made more sense when I supposed the career opportunities would eventually be more significant.

During the first few days in my university halls, I was so shy and nervous that I just sat in my room. I could hear the noise of excited chatter and laughter from the hall kitchens and wondered continually whether I should muster some courage and introduce myself. The amount of standing up, walking to the door, turning around and sitting back down was innumerable. In the end, the worry of rejection and embarrassment was too much. I didn't move from that room.

After two days and nights had passed, a smiley guy knocked on my door and invited me to join the cheery people down the corridor. This hero – my new mate – introduced himself as Dan. I vividly remember that knock at my door. It was such a simple small act, but it moved me to take action and changed my whole trajectory. Cheers Dan, I will be forever grateful to you! That small gesture immediately took away the worry and nerves, and from that point forward, I was a firm member of the group.

My three years at university were fantastic; I built a strong network of friends that are still in my close circle some 20 years on. We had terrific times, great laughs and shared an incredible journey. However, when we graduated three years later, I still felt like there was a void. Something about my psyche, mainly my lack of confidence, lingered. Whilst I had learned to stand on my own two feet, cook, wash, clean and socialise, I still felt like a quiet, unassuming, and nervous individual (setting aside the alcohol-fuelled nights out!). I started to think about what I could do that would push the boundaries. What could put me into a situation that was so far out of my comfort zone, I would have no choice but to be louder, more confident and outlandish.

So, a Holiday Rep it was...

What was I doing??? Oh, God! We have all heard the stories of Britons abroad, the '18 – 30's' and the antics the holiday reps get up to? I was stepping into Gen X's version of the lion's den – quiet, unassuming ME!! While the thought of getting involved with bar crawls, cabarets and events with hundreds of guests filled me with much excitement; it also poured into me an equal amount of frantic dread that would keep me awake at night.

I worked in Fuerteventura in the Canary Islands for two summer seasons and Andorra for the winter season. It was great fun, and from an experience point of view, the two years away were terrific. They showed me that I could push past my own self-limiting beliefs, worries, concerns, and fears. It taught me that I just had to push on through.

Some of the cabaret scenes were simply awful, especially those in which I had to dance. Anybody that knows me personally will be aware that I DO NOT dance. So, dancing in front of 200 plus people who have paid their hard-earned money to watch, was perturbing. The only saving grace was the free alcohol as part of the entry price, meaning that the viewing eyes were perhaps a little blurry to spot any of my many mistakes.

All in all, being a holiday rep was great fun, and the best part is that I met Emma, my current wife of 20 years. (I call her my current wife – it keeps her on her toes!).

I came back to the UK after two years of living overseas. Two years was always the plan, but afterwards, I found that I was now in a quandary about what to do next. Emma knew exactly what she wanted – she wanted to be a recruitment consultant and to stay in sales. Still undecided, I ended up getting a job in recruitment too, working at a recruitment agency based in the centre of Birmingham. It was a great brand and business, and they were growing exceptionally fast. The company was very structured, and after nine months of 'giving it a go', I realised that it just wasn't for me. I felt far too restricted in what I could do, and the journey to get to the offices every day was painful. I had to catch two buses and take a 30-minute walk, which meant the working days were 06.30 am to 9 pm every day. In hindsight, the issues I had with the structure were all mine. It was more the culture shock coming from the holiday rep lifestyle to a defined and structured day. Nevertheless, at the time, it was all a bit too much, and I left.

Afterwards, I became a construction buyer for a landscape gardening company. It was great fun – managing huge gardens of high value, and I oversaw all orders and products to site – working with the management team, the site teams and reporting to the directors.

From there, I moved across to Severn Trent Water, where I became a qualified MCIPS strategic commodity buyer, negotiating multimillion contracts and frameworks. That was a fantastic experience, as it trained me in the art of negotiation. The training was intense, but I enjoyed every minute of it. On the first day of the three-day 'negotiation' course, they filmed us in a faux client negotiation meeting. This exercise was then replicated on day three to see how we had improved. How much we had – I loved it. It gave me great confidence, inspiration, motivation, education and allowed me to think clearly and strategically about sales, buying and negotiation. Again, I will forever be grateful because now, as a recruiter, I feel that the course, the job, and subsequent learning, formed the foundation for approaching my career in sales.

For any of you that have already read my first book, 'Top Biller – The Life of a Recruiter' – you might remember that it was at this point in my life story that I begin working as a recruiter.

I had become increasingly frustrated at Severn Trent Water. Once a contract or framework had been negotiated and agreed upon, after months of work, spreadsheets, research, and meetings, all I got was a pat on the back and handed the next contract. I was desperate for more. I wanted to work somewhere where my efforts and work was rewarded and demonstrated by my pay. Also, by this time, I had watched Emma do so well as a Temp Consultant in recruitment that I wanted to match, if not beat her earnings. This wasn't a misogynistic need to 'be better than my wife', but instead, her progress had inspired me, and I wanted some of it!

However, at the time, I thought I suited the personality of a buyer more than that of a salesperson. I was calm, considered, and preferred to take time to adequately research; I wanted to have all of the information at my disposal before offering an opinion. I was reserved in my approach and never the loudest person in the room. So, I assumed this was quite the opposite of what you might expect from a recruiter or salesperson.

Still, I decided recruitment was what I wanted, and I was selected for an interview with Hays Purchasing & Supply. Being a qualified buyer made logical sense to me to recruit for procurement staff; having worked in the industry and having achieved my MCIPS, I felt that would carry some gravitas.

The first interview went well; I enjoyed the meeting, the offices were lovely, and I could see myself working there. They even asked me to play in the company's five-a-side football team in a charity tournament the following week! Bingo! After my second interview, I was sure I had nailed it and that the job was mine! I was over the moon.

Unfortunately, whilst I thought the second interview mirrored the first interview, the Director disagreed.

"You don't fit the profile of what we are looking for. You're not salesy enough, loud enough, confident enough, or someone that would fit in with the team. I'm afraid you simply don't have the right personality traits to make it work." He advised.

I was devastated. I knew deep down that I could do the role. The recruitment process is simple, right? Find an opportunity, find a suitable candidate and put the two together?! I could do that!

The feeling of rejection was unusual to me – I was used to being offered roles after interviews.

Across the street from Hays P&S was Hays Construction & Property. In a moment of pure adrenaline, I walked over and made an announcement to the manager. Whilst the verbatim of the statement might have morphed over the years, the heart of it remains the same. I said, "Take me on, and I will spend *every* waking hour proving Hays P&S wrong for not giving me a chance!".

That is where it started. That singular point in time is where I believe my personal brand journey began.

CHAPTER ONE

What Makes you Different?

It's important to build a personal brand because it's the only thing you're going to have. Your reputation online, and in the new business world is pretty much the game, so you've got to be a good person. You can't hide anything, and more importantly, you've got to be out there at some level.

— **Gary Vaynerchuk**

When we were kids, most of us shied from the suggestion of being different; it was to be avoided at all costs, and to blend in, was to win. But we are not children anymore, and in this brave new world, where everybody has a platform, our differences become our greatest asset. What makes us different is how we will be recognised. It is also going to be the fundamental tool in our personal branding kit. Knowing what you would like to be known for is crucial. In this chapter

I will discuss how I discovered my differences and then utilised those assets to advance my personal brand.

As we have already established – I was a different breed to your 'usual' recruiter.

I am a strategically trained buyer, spreadsheet savvy, borderline OCD, process, procedure, structured, logical, HIGH C individual.

I am not your typical salesperson.

Don't get me wrong, I could educate myself in sales, practice and submerge myself in the art of the salesman – but would my character traits relate?! Time would tell.

The recruitment industry back in 2006 had issues; the service levels were insufficient, and the feedback from clients and candidates would echo that sentiment. There was never any feedback; consultants would arrive one minute be gone the next, and service continuity was poor. The repetition of meetings and information was constant because the turnover of recruiters was so high. There were trust issues from all parties, and thus, recruiters were 'the bad guys', that would steal from the poor and give to the rich (the recruiters being the rich!). We were deemed to have over excessive margins, and that the candidates were always the fall guy. There was the issue of poor staff placement, charging excessive fees, and then the consultant would run for the hills and hide until the rebate period was over. Recruiters were considered to over promise and under deliver. They constantly let everybody down and provided false information. Just a simple google search on recruiters shows the vast black hole of negativity that fuelled the industry.

And this was before I had even made my first sales call!

Being able to answer the following client's question was my first lesson in recruiting.

"What makes you any different from all of the other recruiters that call me on a daily basis? They all tell me that they are the recruiter of choice. What makes you any better?"

I answered quite simply, "Me – I am the difference."

The only answer to this question is **YOU!**

YOU are the difference.

But – what makes you any different?

Let's discuss the different options that you might have within a personal branding choice. Is having a solid idea of your identity at the beginning imperative or is it about starting and waiting for your brand to hone itself?

This is not my unique philosophy – it was the coaches in the early days of my initial training in recruitment in 2006 who told me that 'what separates you from anyone else is always *you*'. It's about how you work harder, how *you* purposely go out and find the candidates; the ones that other consultants can't find. What differentiates *you* from any other recruitment business and any other recruitment brand is always *you* as an individual.

Social media wasn't particularly big in 2006, and your work identity was not something that was normalised as a personal brand. So, I knew that I needed to find solutions and ways of working that differentiated me from everybody else. I had to tell people, which meant talking to clients and candidates to explain how I worked and what made me different to other recruiters. Back then, we predominantly used the telephone and spoken conversation. These days, as you know, social media has allowed us to put those conversations onto a much broader and bigger platform. It's enabled me to get my message out there faster, but the message is the same as it was in 2006.

As a day-to-day recruiter, my 'brand identity' is about working with my clients and candidates to find the best solutions. That, as a brand identity, has not changed; all that has changed is the format in which I can complement the existing conversations. Before social media, I would tell candidates, "I pre-qualify everyone, to ensure that when I'm putting you forward to a position, it matches what you are looking for."

And I would! I would go out and meet every candidate, and go through all the qualification checks. I would talk through what I do, how the process works, and my overall end goal for them as an individual. I still have that conversation; I still do the one-to-one, face to face meetings, but now I can also use social media to tell everybody what I do. For example, I could post a video on LinkedIn to say, "I'm sat in a car park waiting to meet a great candidate. I can't wait to get to know them a little bit better. I can't wait to find out how I can benefit them, how I can find an amazing opportunity for them to interview for; a position that will change their life and their career for the better."

This approach isn't a pitch; it's simply me telling my network how I work and intentionally telling them that I do the job correctly. The post says, 'I'm genuinely engaged and interested in working with the candidate to find them a new position'.

If I were to go back to 2006, I would meet the candidate, and then I would call numerous clients, one by one, and say, "I've just met this fantastic candidate that X,Y and Z, you really must see them now."

I still do that, but now I have a social media audience, which means my message reaches thousands of people at once rather than one phone call at a time. Now I can post, "I'm meeting a brilliant person who does X,Y and Z. If you've got a role or requirement and they're of interest, you should get in touch."

I'm not telling my audience to do anything; I'm just creating the proposal and the pitch for them to make a decision.

It's important to recognise that the recruitment market back in 2006 is not remarkably different to how it is in 2021. Indeed, the perception of the UK market and industry is the same. The perception of the recruitment market still includes:

- A lack of trust
- Poor service
- A high turnover of recruitment staff within the industry
- High levels of inconsistency
- Poorly trained recruiters
- Service delivery at the detriment of KPIs

This means that the opportunity to be 'different' in recruitment is relatively simple.

Like anything in life and business, you must find the pain points and deliver a solution. Speak to your market and listen to the feedback. Questions you should be asking are:

- Where and what are the issues?
- Where does the service not deliver? Why doesn't it deliver?
- What would you like to happen?
- How would you like me to work with you?

Find the answer to these questions, and deliver on them. Find suitable candidates for quality opportunities, and the rest is relatively simple.

I had a straightforward goal; *to do what I say I will do whilst staying loyal to the cause.* In many ways, my character traits and personality lend themselves to this approach. I like systems and consistency. My biggest fear in life is to disappoint and to not achieve a goal or objective.

I am fiercely competitive but in an honest, hardworking, and strategic way. This is what has set me apart from the rest.

In the beginning, all the recruiters around me were great at relationships, terrific at sales, and excellent at being the loudest person in the room. There were very few, however, that were structured, organised and reliable. This was my edge; this is what made me different.

My structure and organisation are what set me apart. I am never late for meetings or calls, and everything has its place and time. If I said I would call you at 4 pm on Thursday – guess what – you will receive a call on Thursday at 4 pm, and not a minute later.

I delivered on my promises, motivated by the fear of underperforming or disappointing others. This mindset kept me honest, consultative and hardworking. I kept my market well-informed, and thus, I set their expectations early in the process. I simply delivered on my promises— nothing more, nothing less.

The problem with today's recruitment market is that many recruiters feel like they need to say what they deem their clients or candidates want to hear, rather than being honest with them. A consultative and candid approach holds far more gravitas than over-promising and under-delivering. Being unable to back up your promises will make you appear bad at what you do, which gives clients trust issues and is what the recruitment market has sadly become renowned for. I believe this is a flawed approach, and it trickles down across the whole recruitment industry.

I want to change that. I want to be different.

In conclusion, what makes you different could be the one thing that makes positive changes in your industry, or it could inspire you to go for opportunities you never before thought possible. Drilling down to the 'who am I, really?' is one of the most advancing progressions you can make for your business and your personal growth.

CHAPTER TWO

What is a Personal Brand and Why is it Important?

"Personal branding is about managing your name — even if you don't own a business — in a world of misinformation, disinformation, and semi-permanent Google records. Going on a date? Chances are that your "blind" date has Googled your name. Going to a job interview? Ditto".

— Tim Ferriss

A personal brand is essentially the same as any other brand, other than the product, is *you*. Building a personal brand can uncover untold opportunities and enable you to discover more about yourself and what you can achieve. These days, for good or bad, a quick online search can tell you a lot about a person in just a few clicks. A solid personal brand means that anybody that comes across your name will quickly be in no doubt of a) what you do, and b) how well you do it.

The immediacy of this knowledge will allow for more recognition, acceptance, and acknowledgement, making previously tricky introductions easier. In this chapter, I discuss my journey of understanding the potential of building an excellent personal brand and how I eventually stopped dawdling and got on with it!

The 2018 whirlwind

I started as a disbeliever.

I am a procrastinator by nature; I blame my dad for that. I recall a childhood memory of my dad returning to a car showroom over four weeks to look at the same car. On the fifth week, on finding out that the showroom had sold the car, he looked at me in sheer disbelief and disappointment.

"But Dad," I said, "you had several opportunities to commit, and you didn't. Now you're annoyed that somebody else grabbed the opportunity and committed?!"

As illustrated above, I have always been full of wisdom for others, but learning to apply it to myself has been a learning curve.

Looking back to October 2018, I had attended several seminars, open days, networking meetings and mentorship talks which all promoted the benefits of 'going live', recording social media videos and putting out a personal brand. I would shiver at the thought. I remember the speakers saying, "during the break, you need to go outside and record your first video on social media and go live. Tell your network where you are, and what you are doing. You won't regret the impact it will create."

I wasn't convinced; my whole being rejected the mere thought of such a request. There was no chance I would put myself through that sort of emotional torment! What me? With my thick Birmingham accent, talking into my phone whilst walking around a car park? No, there was zero chance of that happening!

However, many people at the seminar did it, and afterwards, they were congratulated. Some of the videos were great and produced by pure naturals. Others I felt embarrassed for. I didn't yet understand what the benefit or value was. Why should I make videos? Why can't I simply write posts and add a photo – that still works, doesn't it? Videos are for overly confident people that have way too much to say, and that, as we know, is *definitely* not me!

The video scenario above wasn't a one-off – these situations happened to me numerous times, and I would always find an excuse not to commit. I would grab an extra cup of coffee, need the toilet, call someone, grab some lunch, or nip back to the car to collect another pad or pen. I was always looking for an escape route or an excuse.

Skip forward eighteen months, and I was still to gain the confidence to make the videos. I could see the benefit, and I believed in the concept, but I lacked the personal motivation to make it happen. I had allowed my inner procrastinator to get in my own way, and I hadn't moved forward or committed.

It was 5:30 am 3rd October 2018. I'd set my early alarm on a warm, sunny Wednesday morning, ready for the two and a half-hour drive down to the Watford head office for the Directors round table meeting. The drive is enjoyable because it's a nice early start and a couple of hours of 'me time'. I was listening to Gary Vaynerchuk and 'Crush It!' on Audible. It's a great listen for anyone that struggles to take action and move things forward. If this is you, then I recommend you grab a copy of the book.

About two hours into the drive, Gary Vaynerchuk says (not verbatim), *"if you are one of those people that doesn't commit or act, and yet procrastinates and makes judgements on others, then it's time to change. Sometimes you have to jump in the pool, even when you're scared! When you own it, put yourself out there and be you, your vibe is going to attract your tribe, and you will be able to make changes in this world"*.

And this was it! His words created the game-changing moment where it finally sunk in. I needed to act! I had spent eighteen months making decisions based on zero commitment; I had used up all the excuses. Now there was no escape, there was no let-up, and there was no one left to motivate me other than me! And that, my dear readers was the moment of truth; the moment the spark was ignited.

Whichever way you get to your goals, it must *be you*, deciding *for you*.

I arrived at Watford; it was about 07.30 am, the sun was beaming down. I walked around the car park a couple of times, and I finally did it! I made my first social media video and pressed 'post'! It was out there. There was no real value or content within the video; but it was me doing something that scared me.

I was delighted with myself in all honesty – I had done it! The comments and encouragement I received on the post were all positive. Then came the comment from a friend, Chris Williams, who wrote, "Well done! I now challenge you to record ten videos in ten days."

I quickly accepted, partly because it created the accountability that I needed, but ultimately because I knew it would benefit my personal development and brand journey. I was terrified nonetheless!

The following ten days contained many highs and lows, but the process allowed me to become more comfortable with making videos and creating content daily. Facing potential ridicule and critique head-on helped me develop as a person and thus grow my personal brand. I will be forever grateful to everyone involved in the process, including the mentors who began to shift my mindset, Gary Vaynerchuk, who made me take action, and Chris Williams for challenging me to the ten videos in ten days challenge.

After the ten videos in ten days, clients and candidates I hadn't spoken to in years got back in touch. I attracted a new market and re-engaged my 'forgotten' market. I built new relationships with new clients and candidates, and I was on everybody's social media news streams and timelines. The market got to know me by understanding my motivators and my ambitions. They essentially got to see the 'whites of my eyes', and this enabled me to build trust and credibility within a public space.

Other recruitment consultants told me that their clients were excitedly talking about me and the videos I was producing. People contacted me, suggesting what my next video should be about, and began sharing their own ideas and which content they would like me to discuss next.

I had my first social media' hater', and it gave me the strength, courage and ability to carry on regardless. The 'hated' video was also the most watched video of the ten in ten video challenge. It's amazing what a divided opinion can do to engagement and interaction. Everyone likes a good bit of aggravation!

It's also worth noting that 'video' engagement statistics are far more reliable than views on a post. Viewers must stay connected with the video for longer to count as engagement, which results in a truer reflection of how engaged your audience is.

In 2018, I believe these videos 'differentiated' me from the rest of the market, and it is still the case now. Few people produce video content as they are fearful of ridicule, objection, and haters – just like I used to feel! Many people are uncomfortable with how they look on camera and how they sound. Even making a small mistake, using the wrong word, or stumbling into a sentence can completely repel people from the desire to create videos. However painful, these are all part of the video creation journey – we all go through it! The video content creators that survive are the ones that push through and carry on regardless. Don't wait for 100% perfection as you will never get there, being 75% happy is my barometer, to get it done and put it out there. Let it go. It only lasts a matter of hours, by which time people move onto the next post, video, photo or fad.

Don't get caught up on one post or one specific bit of content – you don't get to decide what goes viral and what doesn't. Some of the best posts I have written that offered great value absolutely tanked! Others that I didn't think were particularly good skyrocketed!

Don't be like me and wait eighteen months – you can achieve a lot in that time if you just get started!

What is a personal brand?

- **Your Personal Brand is YOU –** It encompasses everything you are as a human, individual, and the overall service you deliver.

- **It's your WHY –** Your personal brand demonstrates what motivates you, what pushes you to achieve new levels of service and targets that were otherwise unattainable. Your WHY is fundamentally why you get up every day, go to work and achieve your goals. It is your life targets and aspirations. It's what propels you to higher levels so that you can retire early and live on that yacht in the Bahamas – (you know – the one you always talk about!).

- **It's your CORE VALUES** – How you behave, treat people, and what you expect in return, should you have any expectation, is central to your personal brand. It is who you are as a being. Your core values are what makes you, YOU.

- **It's your STRENGTHS, your WEAKNESSES** – We all have weaknesses, but are you brave enough to admit them? In my interview preparation conversations with candidates, I tell them they should always be fully aware of their key strengths and weaknesses. What value do your strengths bring, and what advantages would employers gain from offering you a position? Also, it's important to be aware of the areas you need training in and identifying where your skillset is weaker? There is no shame in admitting weakness if you can demonstrate your intention to improve those areas. For example, my weakness was that I always wanted things to be 100% accurate. This is, of course, both a strength and a weakness, but in the real world, most things will never be 100% correct. So, I wasted a lot of time on impossible tasks – striving for 100% accuracy has slowed me down, especially in decision making. I am aware of it now and can make decisions accordingly to counteract this.

- **It's your SKILLS, RESOURCES, EXPERIENCE and KNOWLEDGE** – These are ultimately what makes you, YOU. We've all experienced events that make us who we are. These events shape our thoughts, actions, opinions, views and ultimately help us determine our next move. Our history defines us, and we must be aware of this. We must embrace this fact and be willing to learn to remove bad habits, negative perceptions, or lessons that have taken us down the wrong path. Every day is a school day.

- **It's your MARKET** – Certainly, your output and results will define where you sit within your market in recruitment and sales. Are you well connected and well placed to serve your market in the best possible way? Are you the go-to person in your market? Does your personal brand resonate within the market or sectors that you work in?

- **It's your CLIENTS, CANDIDATES and VACANCIES –** It is your success in finding the best candidates for your clients. It is finding the best opportunities for your candidates and having a high 'fill rate' for your vacancies. This will shape who you are and how well respected you are in the industry.

- **It's how you spend your HOURS, your DAYS, WEEKS, and MONTHS –** I plan my hours, days, weeks, and months meticulously. I know far in advance what my objectives are for the year, month, week & day. I even factor in my 'down-time'. Structuring my days, weeks and months allows for more success, as there is much less wasted time. Make every moment count, even when you are not in the office.

- **It's your GOALS, TARGETS and ACHIEVEMENTS –** If 22 men were running and kicking a ball around a field with no goal posts or nets, there would be a lot of unnecessary running around with zero scoring and zero results. We must make sure that we identify our goals and targets, giving us a 100% better chance of success. Find clarity on what your goals are and make that your motivation.

- **It's your BAD DAYS, GOOD DAYS, SAD DAYS, and HAPPY DAYS –** We learn from everything that happens to us. Life is a school day, and the bad days are as much of a teacher as the good days. We are an accumulation of all our successes and failures. We are made up of all the times we felt rejection and all the times we felt joy. Don't push aside 'negative' emotions or scenarios – they are great gurus; embrace them.

- **It's your ACTIVITY and your JOURNEY –** This is where you make a difference as a recruiter or in any other sales-led business. We all want more revenue, an increase in sales and lead generation.

What does an effective personal brand do?

An effective personal brand can be immensely powerful, and I believe that in recruitment and sales, it is unbelievably underutilised. An effective personal brand will:

- Build credibility and trust
- Allow you to show your strengths and passions
- Offer and provide a platform for you to be YOU to a wider audience every time you create content
- Allow you to attract more candidates and clients
- Elevate you to higher levels and allow you to build stronger relationships
- Work for YOU and compliment your daily activity
- Allow your market to approach you – which brings a warmer call, business opportunity and working relationship

Your personal brand is the differentiator when it comes to standing out from the crowd. Unfortunately, most people shy away from even trying, as they don't see the importance of a strong personal brand until it's too late.

A personal brand is a long game. It's not about putting a post on a social media platform and hoping it will go viral. Ultimately you don't get a say as to which posts will gain attention and which won't. The audience and algorithms effectively choose for you, so stop concerning yourself with that, at least initially.

A personal brand is about consistency, continuity and your ability to keep showing up – even on the days when you don't want to. It's about showing your audience the rough and the smooth and the good and bad days. You need to be true to who you are and be honest about where your journey is taking you. It needs to be measured and strategic, but authentically *you*.

I am still the quiet unassuming individual that sometimes wants to shy away from the spotlight, but I do have a purpose and a WHY, and that keeps me going. So, I grab opportunities and say "yes" because the more people that hear about what I do, the closer I get to reaching my goals.

Once you've started on the personal brand journey, I don't think it's that easy to turn it off. When you see and smell the potential and think about what it can lead to, it becomes addictive. A personal brand launch gives you the opportunity and the platform to springboard into something you could never have dreamed of, and you have no idea who you're going to meet along the way.

Personal branding allows you to catapult yourself into financial success and personal freedom. However, because success and freedom mean different things to different people, you must always remember your WHY – your motivation – for beginning your journey in the first place.

CHAPTER THREE

The Book – My Top Biller – 'The Life of a Recruiter' Story

You have to have a brand to be relevant today, the world has changed. Anyone with a smartphone is now a journalist, you have computers writing articles, how are you and I going to stay relevant today, how is anyone going to stay relevant today, it's your brand.

— Mark Schaefer

M ost people say they have a book in them, but very few ever sit down and put pen to paper. In personal branding, the advantages of having a book are enormous, as overnight, you become 'the person that wrote the book'. That status alone opens many doors for speaking engagements, articles, PR, and most importantly, you are then considered an authority on your book's subject. A quick search online that sees your name next to a book in your field immediately validates you. In this chapter, I will tell you my story of becoming an author and how my whole life has changed as a result. I will explain exactly how I did it, and how to convince you to do the same.

As part of the 2018 whirlwind, I embarked on writing a book that ultimately became a best seller. 'Top Biller – The Life of a Recruiter'.

Overall, the book took about 18 months, from writing the first word to the final published edit. There was a six-month gap in-between where work took over, and I lost the habit of writing.

Christmas 2018 arrived and I decided that I wanted to go a different direction in my career (by September 2019). I was determined to complete the book by then, so that everything could happen together. The thought process, was that my youngest child, Hugo would be going to school (which meant we thankfully dropped the nursery cost – the price of a 2nd mortgage!), and I could use the book as my differentiator. I would become the recruiter that wrote a book. In effect, Top Biller would become my 'business card'. It was never a profit-making idea at the start, but what entailed has been life changing.

'Top Biller – The Life of a Recruiter' is my story of how you can use rejection to fuel your fire. I simply wrote a recruitment book that's relatable to recruiters. I didn't want it to read like a textbook, like many of the others I've ploughed through. I wanted the readers to find empowerment, inspiration, motivation and belief. If I could empower the quiet, unassuming recruiter that always felt they were out-shouted by the noisiest person in the room, then this book can prove that they can also outperform even the loudest person, if they carried the belief.

The final edit of Top Biller was published on November 7th 2019, and the journey of the book began. My network continued to grow, and each day since has surprised me. The process became a very humbling exercise. The momentum continued to build, and by April 2019, Top Biller had sold across 28 countries and reached Amazon No.1 Best Seller in two categories. Reviews were great and averaged five stars on Amazon.

One of the best ideas I had was to add a free 'Month Planner' gift in the back pages of the book. The initial reason was to be nice, friendly and add greater value to the readers. However, the happy consequence allowed each reader to contact me via email and find a reason to relate and engage. Readers would request a copy of the planner, I would oblige, and simply ask if they would kindly add a social media post and write a review on Amazon; most duly did! This small ask became self-perpetuating, and the readers began to market the book to their networks. I continued to respond to all activity – emails, DMs, messages across all social media and always followed up. The messages always showed complete gratitude that someone had spent their hard-earned money on a copy of my book. I answered any questions and helped in any way I could.

Top Biller managed to quickly reach a global audience. At the time of writing, twelve months on, Top Biller has sold more than 5,500 copies worldwide across 44 countries. Social media marketing and the personal brand boost has been the most significant part of the journey and allowed the book to reach thousands of individuals. The feedback has been fantastic, a little surreal at times, but truly humbling. Recruiters have felt motivated, inspired and motivated to either change their habits or have faith that their character traits can be positive, even when they feel like the 'outsider' or the quietest person in the office.

Writing your own book

The book has been one of my most powerful platforms for my personal brand growth, and I wholly suggest you write your own. Sometimes I get detailed reviews on my book, and some are warm, heartfelt responses. I respond to every single one. It's nice to know that I've changed someone's thought process, inspired or empowered them to do something purely by my words. You can do that for others too.

I've made many fascinating connections, even with people that you would think are off-limits. I've also had many interesting conversations with people not looking for anything other than to say, "thank you – you've inspired me today".

I started contacting authors years ago when I was reading a book a week. I would post online about my book of the week, and I would then try and find the author. You'd be amazed at how easy it is to find them. I'd message under their posts, and often they would send me a note to say thank you. It makes you feel happy, and if you've had an emotional connection with the author, it helps to embed the information from the book into your brain. Whatever it was that inspired you is more likely to get nuzzled in the noggin, shall we say?

As I mentioned, the initial idea or concept to write my book was about four years previous, when I was going to property seminars, presentations and training sessions. Rob Moore, from Progressive Property based in Peterborough, has around nine published books, and his business partner, Mark Homer has written a few. The other trainers and coaches within the training sessions had written books too. They were always saying things like, "You've got to get out there and market yourself. Everyone has got a book in them."

I went on a social media training day, and the lead trainer had two books out. The whole circle had at least one! I sat there, thinking, "I could write something." I didn't know what I wanted to write about or what I was going to do, but I knew at that point that I was going to write something!

I was there with my notebook scribbling, "I could document my property journey!" But, quickly realised that I should be writing about recruitment – it is my forte after all. Irrespective of my recruitment experience, I sat there worriedly thinking, "what do I write? How do I make it interesting?"

I ordered two recruitment books off Amazon, and they were dull as dishwater; they were like textbooks. I realised that there was a gap in the market to write something more relatable and easy-going. I knew that if I could write a book, that it could become my business card, if successful and well received. This was an idea that came from reading 'The Key Person of Influence' by Daniel Priestley. He talks about having assets online so that people can find you in a Google search. The book is excellent—Priestley talks about the benefit of having blogs, articles and writing a book. The goal is that by writing, people aspire to be you, and it will elevate your brand to become the 'go to' person in your industry, thus becoming the 'key person of influence'. I thought that if I wrote a book, I'd become 'the recruiter that wrote a book', which would differentiate me from my market. And it did, it worked – it made me stand out! People would say, 'Oh, you need to speak to Steve – he's the guy that wrote Top Biller.'

It was an additional sales pitch. I included many appraisals from clients and candidates in the book and sent those people free copies asking them to post something on social media. I wanted to attract their competitors and contacts within the market. It worked a treat – before I knew it, my old candidates and clients were promoting my book organically. This meant that other people in my industry saw it, and it evokes the thought, "Oh, well if Steve Guest wrote a book, he must know what he's doing."

That's exactly the response that I was looking for!

The other concept behind the book was that I was different. As discussed, I was never your typical recruiter. I also supposed that the other quiet people would be more likely to read books, to take themselves off and desire some personal space. I wanted *those* people to read my book and think differently about themselves. I wanted *those* people to think, "I don't have to be the loudest to be a success. I don't have to be the one that is constantly reminding everyone in the office that I'm the best thing since sliced bread. I can quietly sit here and get on with what I've got to do."

My book journey has been strange and challenging to adjust to. Just the other day, I walked into a training room, and the coordinator announced, "Wow, we have a published author in the room!"

Embarrassed, yet inwardly proud, I quietly sat down at the back of the room. After the session, one of the attendees sent me a message on LinkedIn. He said that the book had spoken to him, as he felt he was never accepted as a 'typical recruiter' either. The message went on to say that the book had inspired him to get back into the thick of it and he couldn't wait to get to work. He said he had rediscovered his mojo, feeling both rejuvenated and motivated again.

Wow – that felt amazing!

I get a lot of messages like this. It's not that the book is incredibly innovative – I'm not trying to redo the recruitment world, and I'm not trying to reinvent the wheel – but I believe that it inspires people because it's a reminder of the basic process, procedure and structure. It allows people to improve, work better, and become more efficient. People that have been in recruitment for a long time sometimes become lazy, or they forget some of the basics (me included!). Those people read the book and think, "I need to reassess the way I structure my day because I've dropped off over the years."

Ultimately, I wanted to inspire. I wanted to empower and prove that the quiet, unassuming individual can still achieve. I wanted it to differentiate me from the rest of the market. I also wanted to create assets that create other income streams. So that is a big tick off the list as the book now generates a monthly recurring income.

Not everybody thought that it was a good idea. When I told my wife, Emma, that I was writing a book about two years prior, she quietly thought it was a bit of an 'ego thing'. After the fact, she admitted that she felt it was my self-importance getting away with me. But when the book went into profit within five months of being published and the revenue started coming in, she quickly changed her thought process.

She is still a little bit embarrassed by the book, as she doesn't do anything by way of social media or personal branding. I think she just thought it was one of my fads and that I probably would never follow through and get to the end. She was quietly surprised when it was successful.

When Emma and I first met, we were opposites; I was the quiet one, and Emma was the loud one, which is where the initial attraction came from. As we've got older, we've balanced out a little, although she's still the spontaneity spirit, and I'm the classic spreadsheet fan! We find terrific equilibrium at work, but in terms of online photos, videos, and anything where she can see herself, she wants no part of it! She's a massive part of my brand, even though she chooses to be largely invisible.

Prior to the publication of Top Biller, I was sat in a three-day social media training event, and the trainer asked the audience of sixty or seventy people, "how many in this group have written and published a book?"

Nine or ten hands went up. As it was a time before Top Biller was published, I didn't offer my hand.

"Keep your hands up if you've sold more than 50 copies?" He continued.

All the hands went down – every single one.

"Oh God, less than 50 copies? Maybe this is a lot harder than I'd envisaged!" I thought.

I found it crazy that people would write a book, not knowing whether an audience existed. Why would you go to all that effort, to then not put in the legwork and make sure an audience will buy it? I sat there, and I wondered why so many of them had failed? I realised in that moment that you've got to bring people along with you on the book journey. You must create a story so that people will want to travel with you and are more likely to spend their hard-earned cash to buy your book. I made it my mission from that point forward to shout about it consistently from the rooftops. It helped the sales fly!

I'd been in the recruitment business for 15 years, and I've been outwardly promoting my personal brand for three years or so. I had over 20,000 connections (at the time), so it wasn't necessarily a surprise when I started marketing the book, people already knew who I was. Still, I'm hugely humbled by its success. The book has been imperative to my personal brand journey, and I would advise anybody to try and do the same thing if they have the desire and means.

There is still a massive gap in the market for recruitment books and trust me – writing a book is a fantastic journey. I think it's useful for self-evaluation and allows you to think about what you want to be associated with.

Everyone has a story, a unique journey of ups and downs. If everyone told their story competently, regardless of the subject matter, each of those books would be interesting.

If half of the people that read *this* book end up writing their own book on recruitment, it could change the way people view the industry. The world might learn that it's not such a fist bump, gold Rolex trade and fancy pin striped suits. It's a trustworthy, hardworking, rewarding and essential industry.

Exposure

So, it's one thing to write a book, but it's essential to have a steady game plan of how it's going to gain exposure. I think I've done remarkably well in that area without a traditional publishing house behind me. Much of the book's success is due to my connections across social media, and secondly by asking readers to contact me for the free planner. I responded to everybody that made a request and asked if they would mind sharing a post on social media and leaving an Amazon review. It worked well and made the journey personable; the readers became involved in my journey and many marketed the book to their network.

The idea of writing a book daunts many people. In the dawn of social media, people don't even write lengthy emails anymore. So, if you're thinking, "I'd love to write a book, but I don't know where to start, and don't think I'm a good enough writer," don't let it stop you!

I wrote Top Biller, and then I approached an editor to add some finesse. I'm not a professional writer, after all. I want to get my point across, but I'll leave it to the professionals to make it more readable. I am always happy to tell people that I worked with an editor and I don't I feel the need to shy away from the subject. In my opinion, it was a smart move! For example, if you needed your plumbing fixed, and you had a basic idea of how to do it, you would likely still hire a plumber to make sure that it is properly fixed. It's the same principle.

Writing a book is a big step, and I never thought that mine would do as well as it did. If you've got a story that you feel will resonate with people, write it! Please don't be worried about potential ridicule, or critique, because it's going to happen one way or another. Also, you might as well go and try and do things that scare you a little bit – the journey is far better than any outcome.

Often, I'll be sitting in the lounge on a Saturday or Sunday night, and I'll get a random message from someone on LinkedIn or Facebook, thanking me for writing the book, saying how good it is, and how it's inspired and empowered them. It's a cliché, but as they say, if you inspire just one person to be better, your job is done.

How I published the book

I self-published my book with Sam Pearce at SWATT Books. I messaged her and told her my book plans, and she arranged a Zoom call and comprehensively explained the self-publishing process. I liked the idea of self-publishing as I always wanted to have full control of the marketing.

I'm a huge advocate for self-publishing. I was keen on the print on demand element as it was going to be available across 7,000 bookstores worldwide, and that people could buy the book anywhere in the world via a printing place that's local to them. The costs also appealed to me as it was a hands-off process. I didn't want to purchase lots of stock and then have multiple trips to the post office. It allowed me to spend more time promoting the book than having to run around posting it.

I buy two boxes of books every month or so, which I use to promote and giveaway. It works! Over 12 months, I've had a continuous social media flow and promotion of the book in various guises; whether a competition, appearing on podcasts, or videos of me celebrating certain milestones. It's been a great way of getting Amazon reviews and relevant feedback from my network.

Many people are intimidated by the idea of writing a book, especially if they believe they need to find a traditional publisher. Many people are uninformed about the benefits of self-publishing, and believe that it hasn't got as much gravitas as traditional publishing. I hope Top Biller is an excellent example that this isn't the case.

How to get ideas

Top Biller's main themes are:

a) You don't have to be a typical recruitment character.
b) Process and procedure equal success.

I sat and thought, "okay Steve, what are the big things that have happened over the 15 years that have catapulted you forward?"

Then the memoir elements started to flow. Once you've got those things down – the dramatic stuff – you have the core concepts along the journey to begin building chapters around.

For me, the big drama, in my career at least, was being rejected and told, "you don't have the right personality to be consultant", and how I proved them wrong.

You need the core elements that make your book about you. That way, your book becomes more personable, and readers will become more engaged with the content.

Many recruitment books I've read in the past have been akin to manuals. In contrast, I ended up with a memoir wrapped up in helpful advice. Anybody writing a book should talk about their journey and not be embarrassed by their stories – they are what make you who you are.

Always be genuine – you're not trying to be the next Nobel Prize winner. Document things in the same way you would on a blog or journal, and don't put much pressure on it becoming a bestseller.

You don't have to write a long book either; something is better than nothing. Many people are making names for themselves with short, 10,000-word business books.

My Top Biller journey has been surprising and has exceeded all expectations. The best part has been personable connection with the readers – it's wonderful to have an impact on so many people. You can do it too.

Just start writing. Start today!

CHAPTER FOUR

The Power your Personal Brand Holds

Your brand is a gateway to your true work. You know you are here to do something – to create something or help others in some way. The question is, how can you set up your life and work so that you can do it? The answer lies in your brand. When you create a compelling brand you attract people who want the promise of your brand – which you deliver.

— Dave Buck

In this chapter, we will explore how being our authentic self and sharing all the trials and tribulations of our journey is a superpower. I'm not kidding; I couldn't believe the overwhelming engagement and positivity I received just by being *myself*. A good personal brand gives you the power to reach new heights, make excellent connections and open previously closed doors. I am going to show you how I did it, and in turn, how you can do it too.

From my perspective, my personal brand's power has come from the willingness to do things that others aren't doing or willing to do. It has elevated me to become the person I wanted to be, and put simply, people will be more likely to listen to what I have to say. Although we define our personal brand, equally, our personal brand defines us. It becomes a lot clearer to convey the right message over time, especially if you keep turning up with regular posts promoting a consistent message and ideology. The key messages become more coherent. A personal brand gives you focus, it gives you drive, but it also gives your audience clarity as to what you're doing. It tells them who you are, what you stand for, how you work, and what your ethics are. It allows people to approach you, because your brand precedes any introduction or initial conversation. If you get the personal brand right, then it's only going to build and enhance your credibility.

Many people have created and forged successful careers using a solid online presence. If you think of Gary Vaynerchuk, his whole brand *is* his social media presence and journey. Just like him, building a successful personal brand will help you to experience more opportunities as more people learn who you are and where to find you. Personal branding has helped me grow my career in numerous ways and allowed me to diversify; not just concerning recruitment but also growing a coaching and mentoring program. It's allowed me to sell more books and gain more listeners to my podcast. All the endeavours link together and are self-perpetuating.

Personal branding attracts partnerships. It helps to generate more sales, it improves credibility, it increases online influence, and helps to secure work. It has enabled me to grow my career in directions I couldn't have imagined, and opened up multiple opportunities and relationships. It has also facilitated my personal development when I started surrounding myself with new people looking to be a part of the journey, as they could also see opportunities for themselves within my personal brand.

The power of the personal brand is that it can be authentically *you*. You develop a consistent message, define your audience, and begin to create a path that you wish to be known for. All this combined allows you the clarity and focus to craft your brand vision.

Fifteen years ago, when I first started in recruitment, it was always about the company brand. Hays was a market leader – and one of the largest recruitment agencies in the world. So, when individuals came to me as a consultant at Hays, it was because, generally, everybody knew *them*, not *me*. Now, the impact of social media has pushed the personal brand to the forefront, and we can have the same power as the company brand used to hold. Utilising personal brand and company brand together can be immensely powerful.

Consistency

It takes 20 years to build a reputation and five minutes to ruin it. If you think about that, you'll do things differently.

Warren Buffett

But is that true?

As I write this, Piers Morgan has just resigned from his popular morning TV show – 'Good Morning Britain', over some salacious words he used about the Oprah Winfrey, 'Meghan and Harry 2021' interview. He is well known for speaking his mind, but it appears he has taken it too far on this occasion. However, he has stuck to his guns, and his personal brand is strong. I am in no doubt that he will bounce back more vital than ever. That's the groundwork and personal brand he has built. His followers are devout.

Anybody that brings disruption, in whatever form, will always interest people. A divided opinion; whether you agree, or you disagree is often tantalising, and many people want to make their comment or their opinion known on social media. Online forums allow people to have more confidence than they would do face to face, although I suspect that very few of the opinionated keyboard warriors, would sit in front of Piers Morgan, face to face, and argue with him. He's lived a life of being hated and ridiculed as an individual when he worked at the newspapers, but he stands strong.

Personal branding allows people to find that inner confidence. Piers Morgan, love him or hate him, is confidently true to who he is. He knows he could stand in a room and divide it right down the middle.

I am quite the opposite of Piers Morgan, as I'm mostly respectful and thoughtful, but the point remains, in one way, we are the same – both of us are *always* consistent in our personal brand.

It is in my opinion that people gravitate to the people that are generally outspoken in their market, and whether you consider yourself an influence or not, if you are on display, people will come to you for reassurance. We are all human. We all have good and bad days, yet most people don't show reality on their social media, and much of it is tailored to that perfect photograph or perfect family scene. We all know it's not fully authentic, and it doesn't speak to us in the same way as someone who is being 100% real. If you're going to work on your personal brand and show your journey, it must be relatable. If you show weakness and the bad days, other people can come to you and ask, "what did *you* do to get through it?"

Vulnerability and authenticity build a connection.

Most of us gravitate to authentic people that say, "you know what, some days you can feel a bit crap. Some days it does all fall apart. Some days you don't want to go into work." It helps us to feel that our own lives and struggles are validated.

Indeed, in recruitment, fear of showing weakness is rife because recruiters are expected to be seen as 110% motivated every day of the week. It's such a high octane, high energy job, that showing any weakness will be deemed as under-performance, and it will be questioned if the recruiter can't hack it.

I've managed people in the past who admitted they felt they couldn't speak to me about their problems. When I found that out, I was disappointed in myself, and it became something I wanted to change – especially as a coach and mentor. It's one of the reasons I set up the 'Free Recruitment Mastery Facebook' group (https://www.facebook.com/groups/recruitmentmasteryfree). The group is a collaboration, and we have hashtag days; for example, we have #ranttuesdays #collaborationwednesday and #winnersfriday. #ranttuesdays is where you can let out your frustrations and say what's going wrong that day or week. #winnersfriday is a day we discuss where and how everybody is finding their success. Everybody in the group cherishes the opportunity to show both the positives and negatives of their journey, and I have found a great deal of joy in bringing all of those people together. The fact that the Facebook group is growing and my book has sold so many copies prove there is a market for mentorship and a need for connection. I get daily messages asking, "can I grab you for five minutes – I'm after some advice. What would you do with X, Y and Z situation? How would you handle this? Can I pick your brains?".

It demonstrates that people need an outlet, an accountability partner, and someone to go to when in need of help. That is the power of the personal brand – I can be all of those things to those people. Put simply, if I wasn't constantly putting my journey into the public eye, nobody would know who I was and how I could help them.

My network is much larger and more active than when I first launched Top Biller, and the book sold so well because of the personal brand story that coincided with it. My audience is engaged because they followed me through the highs and lows of writing my first book, the launch of the program, the launch of the Facebook group, the rise in my personal brand, and my stark honesty about getting through the pandemic. The people that have followed my journey feel a part of it, and are thus invested in what follows.

Sharing the journey holds power, and the personal brand is the result.

Defining the brand

You mould your brand as much as the brand moulds you. You share your journey to make it compelling to other humans. If it isn't relatable, if it isn't enticing, and if it doesn't have any definition, it won't be engaging. Your audience is key in helping you define it. I've spent a lifetime trying to find pain points and subsequently offering solutions to them. The pandemic made me realise that one of the main pain points with recruiters was a lack of training. As a response, I launched the online '12 Week Recruitment Mastery Program'.

The Free Recruitment Mastery Facebook Group was born out of the copious amounts of questions and messages I would receive on a daily basis asking for help, support and guidance – I felt that creating a collaborative, free group where other experienced recruiters could field some of the questions, would reduce the growing expectation on my part but also allow for healthy debate and collaboration, globally – which is exactly what its achieved.

Building a personal brand is brick by brick by brick. You continue to define the personal brand at different junctions along the road as opportunities pop up and pain points pop out.

For me, as a result of the Facebook group, it became quickly apparent that everyone within the community was struggling with business development and making sales calls. During a global pandemic with everybody working from home, business development becomes a little trickier. No one is where they should be; you can't just call the office number and be put through.

So, I created the '4-day business development challenge' off the back of what the Facebook group members said. Many of the members left comments saying how much they appreciate the group and that I'd brought everybody together.

It's not difficult to set up a Facebook group – anybody can do it – and although it can be time-consuming, you should see it as another long-term journey. I could have sat there and thought after two weeks, "I've only got 200 people in there. Is there any point?".

Now, five months later, we have over a thousand people. Wow! Plus, the members are engaged because it's not a pitch fest, it's a supportive group where people can get to know each other and help one another.

I've kept it as a space to add value, asking:

"What's happening out there?"

"Where do you need some help?"

I offer day plans and charts that people can use and interact with one another. From a personal brand perspective, it allows me to see what the preliminary inquiries are. So, when I produce social media content or branding content, I can start answering the questions I know need answers because I have a 'pain point front-row seat'.

I believe that the way people interact within the group reflects how I communicate with people. In effect, because they're mirroring the Steve Guest brand, it proves that my personal brand is having some impact.

The fundamental basics of my personal brand are consistency, process, and integrity. When I look at all of the facets that have sprung into being from my personal brand journey, I believe that they all reflect those basics.

Give more than you take

With your personal brand and your social media activity there should be more give than take. If you're going into building a personal brand with the mindset that you're going to 'beat the competition', you'll probably end up failing as you'll be deemed to be pitching all the time, which no one likes long term. Instead, your personal brand is about being bigger and better than your revenue stream. Yes, there are monetary by-products along the way, but trying to solve problems and issues, create solutions, add value, and make people think differently is where you begin to be influential. It's about being genuinely honest and authentic along the way, and I think the more you can do that, the more you can help people. The bigger the mission, the easier the journey.

The more people that are engaged inspires me to learn, develop, and build. Many people in my Facebook group have been in recruitment longer than I have. Some of them will have a bigger audience than me, and I know I don't know all the answers. I'm certainly not where I want to be yet, and there are other people out there that are better at certain aspects of what I do. I'm not so full of ego that I think I know it all, but I offer my educated view and then respect what other people say. I even hope they can sway me!

Stay humble

The worst three words in the English language are "I know that!".

My personal brand has included a great deal of personal development. It's allowed me to consider things I would have otherwise not thought of. The more you surround yourself with engaged people, who are experienced and knowledgeable in the markets you work within, you become far more effective.

It's important to stay humble. If you've formed an opinion, it means that you no longer hear all the factors associated with the matter at hand. I believe that opinions can be dangerous. Although you can't be on the fence about everything, we must not close ourselves off to other people's perspective of the world. Before this journey, I wouldn't have networked with certain people because they didn't serve me, but now that I am on this journey, I realise that anybody could be beneficial to me, and vice versa for various reasons. I've opened myself up to lots of different people with different life experiences. You've got to be genuinely interested in what people say around you, take it on board and ask yourself what parts you resonate with. "What parts do I disagree with? Why do I disagree with it?" etc. This can open a healthy debate and increase engagement.

When I was in my negotiation training at Severn Trent Water, the trainer gave me an example that has stuck with me. He picked someone in the room and put a flat hand in front of their face.

"What do you see?" he asked the participant.

"Your hand".

"What parts of my hand specifically?"

"I can see the back of your hand, your four fingers, a thumb and your knuckles." Said the participant.

"Can you see my nails?" Asked the trainer.

"Yes," said the participant.

"But what you see is different from what I see – I see the palm of my hand. I don't see any nails. I don't see the backs of my knuckles, but it's still a hand, right?" Said the trainer.

"Right"

"The description is different, but we are still discussing a hand." Said the trainer.

This small experiment shows that you can have a different viewpoint or perspective from another party, but the conversation subject or object is still the same. Differing views doesn't make a topic null and void.

Putting yourself in other people's shoes and seeing things from different angles is an undervalued part of the intellect. To see from other people's perspective is an empathetic trait that will appeal to your personal brand's audience. If somebody expresses an opinion that is opposed to yours, in that second, put yourself in their shoes, strip away your ego, and see where they're coming from. You might still disagree with them, but you might learn something about how humans operate, and you will personally develop as a result.

Begin with the acceptance that not everyone is the same as you or me. I had to learn that some people move at a much different tempo to me, which is okay.

My brain works logically, in a step-by-step motion, but most of my peers and colleagues are the complete opposite. I recorded a podcast with James Osborne, Chairman of The Recruitment Network group.

They have two and a half thousand recruitment businesses globally on their books, so he's constantly talking to recruiters. As you know, I've made a career of saying that I am the opposite of a 'normal' recruiter because I follow a set path or set process. He said something to me that I had never thought about before:

"The trouble with grabbing that loud, flamboyant recruiter and telling them to follow a set process & procedure is that – sure – they could probably do it if you KPI'd them to the max, but it wouldn't take long before they get bored. By making them do things your way, you take away their fun, their personality and 'flair'. With processes like yours Steve, some personalities will switch off, and they will leave the job. They don't want to be tied to a desk, ticking all the boxes."

I'd never had it put to me like that, and it made me think.

It's about finding a balance.

A flamboyant recruiter can add an element of strategy or plan, and they would be better for that. Still, trying to change their character traits from a confident relationship-building person into a strategic process, procedure person is not something they would want to do, even if I sell all the benefits. It withdraws who they are as a person. Remember that we all perceive the world differently, but that doesn't mean that you should change who *you* are.

So, there you have it. A personal brand is a hugely powerful tool for exponential growth. There may be times along your journey where you lose speed and want to quit (I know it crossed my mind at the beginning and a few times inbetween). Don't do it! Stay on the train and remember that a great personal brand really is a superpower.

CHAPTER FIVE

Social Media – The Power of Consistency

Start by knowing what you want and who you are, build credibility around it and deliver it online in a compelling way.

— Krista Neher

H ere, I will show you how I have taken my lifelong philosophy of championing consistency and applied it to my personal brand journey. As with pretty much anything, without consistency, you will simply end up wasting your time. I will show you how being consistent in my personal brand has sped up the success and constantly kept me on everyone's timelines and at the forefront of people's minds.

At the beginning of this journey, social media statistics didn't make a lot of sense to me. Building up my social media flair has been a huge learning curve, and at times it can leave you feeling deflated. You must, however, continue marching on.

I feel it's essential to show all the ups and downs of your journey, even though many people don't feel comfortable sharing their vulnerable side. Towards the end of this chapter, I have included excerpts from my journal to help you realise that we all must start somewhere. I highly suggest journaling your own story.

After the journal in this chapter is a social media challenge that I rolled out recently to my network. Why don't you try it for yourself? All the info needed is at the end of this chapter.

How to get started with social media

Ideally, you should do eight-ten social media posts a week. Two a day; one in the morning and one in the afternoon – you're trying to catch people when they're at their desks, and generally, people will surf the internet before they start work, over lunchtime and towards the end of the day. The biggest struggle with posting is knowing what to post or what kind of content you should create. It's essential at the beginning to realise that you are not about to make the world's next viral post. Instead, you're looking to appear on someone's timeline consistently. When that person has a need or a requirement, the first person they think of will be that person who keeps turning up on the timeline. The aim, therefore, is to get that person to think of you the moment they have a need.

The 70/20/10 split

The 70/20/10 split is about consistency.

The idea is that you slowly build up the knowledge around your subjects. I've taken this ratio and used it for my social media and personal branding content. 70% is all about my market – my specialism. It's about what I want my social media to do for me. For example, I want people to know that I'm a specialist commercial construction recruitment consultant targeting the West and East Midlands. I want people to know which vacancies I have, who I represent and which candidates I'm working with.

If there are discussion points that can divide opinion within my sector or market, I can put them out. So, if I'm doing ten posts a week, seven posts will be the 70% central core – the business and the market and sectors I specialise and work in. The business element of my social media.

The 20% or two posts a week, are about me as an individual and what makes me human. It's what makes me different. It's what happens when I wake up, and I feel like crap, or when I feel demotivated. It might be what happens when I've had a fantastic week or what I get up to outside of work. I might post about my reading book for the week, my personal development. What have I enjoyed or been grateful for that week. These posts are relatable and express; 'I'm a person too and not a pushy salesperson'.

The last 10%, or one post a week, is about what's trending for the week. The big topics – what everyone is talking about. At the time of writing, war veteran Sir Tom Moore has recently passed away; a sad story as last year he bought a nation together. Stories like this compel people to be involved and offer comments and/or opinions.

Internationally/nationally trending posts

From a purely social media and strategic point of view, the idea behind trending posts is that they are there to engage. The posts that get decent engagement generally brings along some idiots, but that's fine. Engagement is engagement. Somebody commented on my Tom Moore post, saying that it was all a 'conspiracy'. I left it there, as it divided opinion, and people are entitled to their opinion, even if I personally found it moronic. I suppose it goes back to the philosophy of, 'you're not winning until you've got a hater'. If people are engaging with you even in any manner, it's still going to have some effect. I want some of my posts to divide opinion and create debate because it makes the post trend higher.

Dividing opinion also entices people to your page, as they want to see what else you will do. The interesting thing with the Sir Tom Moore post, is that people engaged with me who haven't liked or commented on my posts for years. It made me think, "What else have you been seeing?"

It reminds you of the people you've forgotten about, and it shows that people do see what you do, even if they don't interact. I call them 'the lurkers'! This is a problem, from a recruitment social media perspective, as people see, follow, and watch but don't get involved. I'm not expecting people to react to job adverts or candidate profiles because most people don't want to advertise that they're either looking for work or they're looking to recruit, as they know every man and his dog will chase them.

So, the point of the 70/20/10 split is that depending on the different kinds of posts you make, it encourages engagement from different types of people and industries.

Much of my network on LinkedIn are construction-related commercial people, and if I put a post out to say, 'I'm looking for a Quantity Surveyor in Birmingham for a Main Contractor to start on Monday,' many will be afraid to be seen interacting. Currently, the market is insecure, and many companies are struggling. There are lots of people out of work and feeling insecure that are looking for a new role. I can change that perception by putting out a post which every contact I have within construction and commercial construction can engage with, and it will help me to fill positions quicker. For example, I recently made a social media post detailing my current opportunities, and within an hour of the post, I had arranged two interviews. It shows me that I have an engaged and dedicated audience in the market I recruit for.

I received a private LinkedIn message yesterday.

"Steve, I could do with speaking to you – we're in the market for someone. Let me know when you're free tomorrow."

I had never met or spoke to this person before, but they were in my network. I called him and he told me that they had a new job as a Branch Manager for a company I knew, but hadn't recruited for in about eleven years or so.

It was out of the blue, so I asked, "out of interest, why did you send me a message on LinkedIn, bearing in mind we've never spoken before?"

"Because you're so active on LinkedIn, and it looks like you are busy in terms of commercial roles. We can tell you've been recruiting in the market for a long time, you're clearly good at what you do, and you seem to be the person to go to," he said.

That conversation alone was a result of me posting and continuously stating, 'this is what I do!'.

So, I got a new client, a new contact and a new vacancy in a difficult market by utilising consistent social media strategies. My social media tasks are all about consistency, and constantly turning up and putting posts out.

Victories and wins

I usually do a post on a Friday to say, 'it's been a great week, registered eight new vacancies, five interviews, couple of offers and a placement.'.

It's providing my market with an update to say, 'I'm doing what I need to do. If you've got a vacancy or you're looking for a new role, you should come to me because I'm successful.'

This personal post is showing my network that, 'I had an excellent week, stayed motivated every day, achieved all my goals and targets that I set out to do. I'm looking forward to the weekend.' ...this is important because, if you don't show the world you are successful and doing well – who will? You've got to put yourself out there and promote. This isn't a sales pitch its simply showing & celebrating your victories and successes.

Business and industry trends

If, like me, you work in construction, I recommend you do a Google search for 'top headlines in construction' or 'journal headlines in construction'. Professional Copywriters get paid a fortune to write enticing headlines & to grab custom from people looking to buy the issue of the publication. Look for the thought-provoking headline, the one that has a 'hook' and that will challenge people to read it. Use the headline, add your own value and content, and include a call to action. Lead your network to engage with your post. The call to action can simply be:

'What do you think?'

'Do you agree?'

'What are your thoughts on this?'

'Let me know in the comments below'

It opens a conversation within the industry and allows potential clients and candidates to make comments or offer opinions without threatening their employment status.

An important note to make here is to not add the link or directly share someone elses written post or article directly onto your timeline – if you do, you will send your engagement or network to 'their' article. You want to capture the engagement on your post not someone else's. You need to manage this as such; by all means add the link to the full article or post in the comments, but don't add it into your text and direct your traffic somewhere else.

Positive quotes

When I first started, and I used to struggle with content. I figured that if I gave myself ten posts to do a week, I could do 'positive quotes Thursday', which took one post away from my quota. All you need to do is find 30 positive quotes, and that's you sorted on a Thursday afternoon for 30 whole weeks! It takes a bit of the pressure off. People love quotes – I know I do! I love asking people for quotes as well. If a quote is positive and inspires, people are more likely to interact with the post and engage with it, the post and engage with it, (use a social media post scheduler to set your posts up so that you don't have to remember!)

Engaging content

My colleague Tom made a post a couple of weeks ago on how you drink your tea. It grabbed a lot of engagement! The post is simply an image of eight cups of tea, from one being a 'borderline tea' with no milk, to one that was almost all milk! Indeed, it engages the public, especially in the UK because we all have an opinion on how we like our tea, and it's fun! It's clickbait, sure, but it attracted the audience.

I'm always looking down my timeline for posts that have a considerable engagement to borrow their ideas. When I was promoting Top Biller, I ran a couple of competitions, inspired by Daniel Disney, who wrote 'The Million Pound LinkedIn Message' (and the foreword to this book!). I messaged him to ask if I could use his posting style, message and content to help promote my book in the same way. He was flattered and agreed, which was so kind and beneficial! If you don't ask, you don't get.

All the information I have accumulated about content has been a matter of trial and error and observation. Many people get wrapped up in the fact that their posts must be perfect and have vast amounts of value and content to gain engagement. Some people spend hours writing a post that doesn't get any traction, and then they sit and think 'what a waste of time that was! Not one person has reacted to my post!' It's important to realise that you're not in control of how the market reacts to the content that you put out. You can't determine the value. Sometimes it doesn't have to have any value at all – some posts can mean absolutely nothing. One of my most prominent posts last year was:

'What's the problem with LinkedIn at the moment, it's all gone a bit haywire?'

The engagement went crazy! There was no value in the post; it was just me having a bit of a rant because I couldn't do what I needed to do on LinkedIn.

People often ask me if they should use photos on their posts. I say yes and no – you should do a mixture of everything because the algorithms are constantly changing. Try posts with no picture; try posts with an image or a meme. Make some posts with videos, and some with competitions or polls. You never know which ones are going to work and which ones are not, so try and mix it up during the week; you'll soon see which ones are gaining more engagement than others. Try things like splitting your sentences with spaces in between. Some people are more likely to engage in something if they can speed read the gist of a post. If you write a long paragraph and all the sentences are joined together, many people won't read it simply because it looks too long-winded & narrative. If you can grab them with one sentence, they're more likely to stay on the post and read the rest.

Unfortunately, you don't get to decide how your market engages, or what they will find interesting or engaging. Some will prefer text. Some will choose to watch you on video. Some would like to see your face so they can relate to what you're saying. Everybody's different. While this may seem like a scattergun approach, it's pretty measured in the 70/20/10 model.

Don't pitch, define

I had a great conversation with a fantastic copywriter. He explained that nobody likes a salesperson, and nobody likes being sold to or pitched at. For example, **don't** do this:

"I'm looking for a great Quantity Surveyor." or "I'm working with this great contractor that is looking for a QS."

Most often, we don't write posts for the very person we are trying to attract. It would help if we write something that engages the audience we are looking to entice. So instead, **do** write:

"Are you an experienced Quantity Surveyor looking for a new, fantastic role this year? Are you struggling with your day-to-day commute? Are you finding that you've outgrown the people around you and you're looking for that step up?"

The way this is written is providing an opportunity.

Another example of how **not** to do it:

"If you need a great Senior Planner, I'm just about to meet one. You need to either ring me or email me now."

That's a sales pitch.

Instead, **do** write:

"I thought I'd grab a couple of minutes. I'm sat in a service station car park. I can't wait to meet this fantastic candidate and go through all the prequalification, get to know them as an individual, understand their needs and understand where they're wanting to take their career. I can't wait to represent them in the market and see what opportunities I can find."

That's not a sales pitch.

That's excitement about meeting a candidate and subliminally I'm saying, 'I do my due diligence. I pre-qualify my candidates. I take the time to get to know them and find out what they're looking for on the basis that I can find them their next exciting position.'

From a candidate's perspective, they should be thinking, "This consultant goes out and meets people to understand who they are and what they are looking for."

And from a client perspective, they should be thinking, "This consultant goes out and meets these candidates and gets a predefined list or target or action plan of what to do with them. Maybe we should put our job role with him as well!"

That message says 'I do what I say I do on a day-to-day basis. This is how I go about it and how I conduct myself'. And bravo, you're the consultant of choice because you do things properly, honestly and ethically while still pitching but not actively pitching.

It's the art of selling without selling.

On this note, I would like to offer you a FREE GIFT. Please follow the link or email address below for a free PDF of the 50 best LinkedIn posts templates to get you started.

http://bit.ly/Personalbrandstory or steve@sguest.co.uk

As promised, I have included excerpts from my journal. I hope it helps you realise that we all must start somewhere. I highly suggest journaling your own story, which I delve into in greater detail in Chapter 8 – Journaling.

At the end of this chapter is a social media challenge that I presented to my network. Why don't you try it for yourself? It will help put much of what we've discussed in this chapter into perspective. Good luck!

My Journal

29th November 2019

Friday has arrived! It's been a busy week – full of ups and downs, offers in, offers turned down. New clients, jobs in – overall, it's been a good week.

Whilst writing this, I am sat in my car (1hr 30mins early!) ready for the Instagram Impact Academy with Chris Taylor – having won a free 1-day training course. Excited to see what it's all about and how I can use Instagram to make an impact.

What am I looking to gain? An impact, a creative edge from another element of social media that I don't use. Perhaps another avenue to create a sales function or stream for the book or make an additional area to build the personal brand & continue to add value.

To even get here has been something else today. It's been a logistical nightmare as Emma had planned a day out, and I was meant to be doing the school run. Instead, Emma has been great in that she is now dropping the boys to me at the end of the course (4.30 pm), and then tomorrow morning, she will collect them from me and take them home. All of this to make it work – sometimes that's what it takes. The easier option would have been to cancel my attendance and give my apologies. Sometimes you just say yes and work a solution to grab the opportunity.

Impact Instagram Academy was tremendous and opened a new line of social media for me. Stories, hashtags, competitions, style, content and value. Chris Taylor delivered value and offered a new way of working!

17th February 2020

I ran a LinkedIn competition on Friday for Top Biller, which worked well – your chance to win 3x signed copies – decent response, so I ended up sending out seven copies to individuals that had gone above the others in the post. One guy tagged everyone in his office (20+ consultants!) Over-deliver and under promise – that was the decision behind giving more back.

9th March 2020

There have been many social media posts at this stage, and I am currently set at 49 positive amazon reviews – but most reviews are from 'paying' customers. It's so tough to promote and keep the marketing going – it is a constant battle to respond to everyone and get traction from interested parties. I work on the basis that it only takes one person to make the book go viral, one post to suddenly and dramatically increase the potential & exposure. So, I continue in an endless pursuit to achieve more and rest in the hope that along the way, the support will grow and the sales will come.

17th April 2020

So, I recorded the 'Recruitee' podcast today – based over in Amsterdam – an excellent interview with some challenging questions where I felt I could add value – lasted about 30mins with a view that the podcast will go live in May.

The Entrepreneur Truth podcast is now Live and doing very well – reaching no.8 in the podcast chart during its first week. I'm confident of seeing some traction with this as the guests are of certainly high calibre and are all winners in their respective fields – looking forward to seeing how that goes.

Hishem Azzouz contacted me today asking for me to be a part of his podcast – he wants it to be an interesting chat about the book, how we can motivate and keep consultants' working momentum and show value along the way. Booked in for 29th April – lots of interesting points made in our initial phone conversation, so looking forward to the chat

Today was also a very significant day for new contacts. I received a LinkedIn message from Catherine Byers Breet, a lady based over in the US and someone who hosts a LIVE US show that would be keen to get me involved. She wants to discuss the book and how recruitment consultants can make the most of the lockdown and create income from other sources – i.e. CV help, guest speaking, career coaching, interview help. – 1st initial call booked for Monday 20th April. It should be an interesting one and indeed targets the US / Canada market – Catherine also has her own YouTube channel, so it should be interesting.

26th June 2020

A day of Strategy calls again today – and going round the globe, I have got UK, Australia, South Africa & US......a fantastic day of calls and getting to add value around the world!

Yesterday I hit the milestone of 3,000 followers on Instagram. So, I have started a Prize Giveaway and copied a very well-

> *received book giveaway post to see if I can emulate the results – the post in question had 1746 likes and 305 comments, so we will see how we get on.* ☺

The Business Development Challenge

Day 1 – Personal Brand / Social Media Day

Take some time to think about you and your personal brand & what you want your social media message to be:

- What are you looking to achieve?
- How do you want your market to see you?
- What does your market already know or think about you?
- What are your core values – what do you hold true? What makes you, YOU.
- How do you differentiate personal brand vs company brand – is it the same?
- Are you restricted to what you can and can't post?
- Share great content – don't pitch or sell!

TASKS

- Minimum of 8 social media posts (Mon – Thurs)
- Exceed expectation ten social media posts (Mon – Fri)
- Morning post – between 8 am – 9.30 am
- Afternoon post – between 12 pm – 2 pm
- A mixture of plain text, text with photo/meme and video – see what's working, test and test and test
- If you have never done a social media video before

- 1st video is essential this week, so plan it in 30 seconds intro
- If you do it – put the link in this group so we can support you & tag me in

Social Media 4 Day Strategy is this

- 70% / 5 posts – Business, market, sector-related – Job ads, sector or market news,
- 20% / 2 posts – Personal – about you – what motivates, core values, the reason why, good & bad days, motivation, ambition.
- 10% / 1 post – What's trending – pick a topic to discuss, not religion or politics.

Content ideas:

- Work or industry stories
- Victories/wins
- Vacancies
- Candidate specs
- Testimonials
- Career / job-seeking advice
- Interview tips
- Business/industry trends
- Trending topics
- Positive Quotes
- Read of the week
- Gratitude posts

LIVE Video discussion points:

Social Media posts and personal branding is about the consistency of message, consistent of 'keep showing up, it's about continuity – getting to a point where you are the first name that people think of when it comes to your specialism, market or location.

It needs to be built into your everyday marketing as more people are now working from home, remote working and online. Personal Branding and social media are integral to building strong relationships and developing your business.

Think of it along these lines – every post on social media can get in front of your whole market – 1 message, written once and submitted, can be seen and read countless times by your market- this is in comparison to making calls – 1 call is only ever to 1 person.

- It's essential to have a social media strategy & consistency in posts, message, sell and brand
- Don't pitch, define
- One message to many, instantly
- Social media posts work in the background whilst you can conduct all other forms of business development
- Super targeted
- You don't know what your network know – who knows who & what
- The impact of video – the relevance of the views
- Video/posts help to break down the seven touchpoints of building a working relationship
- Social media / personal brand is a journey – you won't go viral in a day!

Good Luck with the challenge, and feel free to contact me and let me know how you get on with it:- steve@sguest.co.uk or via any social media channels (Social Media Links in Conclusion Chapter) – always happy to be tagged into any posts you would like me to get involved with.

Getting started with posting on social media can leave you scratching your head, wondering where to start. I hope that learning from my journey and using the tools I have provided will give you a starting point so that you, too, are consistently on your audience's timeline and in their thoughts.

CHAPTER SIX

How to Grow Your Network

My network is *everything*. Without an audience, there would be no point in trying to market anything at all! *A good network is crucial to your success*. Most successful people are expert networkers, and you must become one too (don't worry, it's not as daunting as it sounds!). Before I grew my personal brand, I believed that I was an excellent networker, and in all truth, with the limited tools I had, I was. However, since I embarked on my personal brand journey, my network has grown exponentially, and I have shocked myself. Here I will tell you how I grew my network and how you can too.

In a nutshell, you should grab *any* opportunity and go for it. Manage the risk and make things happen. Fundamentally, the easiest way to grow your network is to keep showing up, stay consistent and have a clear focus of who your audience is and who you want to attract.

It takes effort, hard work and patience – you aren't going to go viral overnight; you aren't going to be an internet sensation in a week. It takes time, with targeted content and a dedication to build. Growing your network is a continual journey.

It's essential to connect with people that engage with your content and your journey, whether it's good, bad or indifferent. Whether they agree or disagree with you, it's always good to acknowledge any engagement. Often the people within your network that might have a contrarian view or a different approach to you, can allow the post to be more engaging to a broader audience. As discussed in the last chapter, if you can create a post that divides opinion and attracts people to debate with the post, it becomes more exciting and can help you expand your network. I've worked with recruiters that have said explicitly that they only network or accept connections from people within their market. I knew a guy who only connected with engineers, so his network was purely engineers. To a certain degree, I understand his reasoning because he didn't want people to come in and cloud what he thought was a valuable list. However, the problem with that approach is that you don't know why somebody is looking to connect with you until you've connected with them. Sure, you'll probably never hear from them again, or they might engage in a few posts that are specific to them, but until you engage, you don't know why they're wanting to connect. It could be that their wife or husband is an engineer and they aren't on LinkedIn, or maybe they're doing a bit of marketing on behalf of someone else. The person connecting might be a PA to an MD for a business that's relevant but you won't necessarily know until you connect and engage.

Helping others to help you

I put out a list of seven opportunities last week, and they were quite a mix! There was a Purchasing Manager, a Design Manager, a Project Manager and a Surveyor – all rather different roles. In the end, 14 people within my network shared the post, even though none of those people were relevant to the roles I'd advertised. Regardless, it went out to all of those individuals' wider networks and the positions were filled.

It's a valuable way of advertising as it's not pitching and 'selling' the opportunities I have to offer. It's a way of growing your network by getting your network to promote what you do, and this will happen when your network is engaged. The further-reaching my posts can go, the easier the marketing becomes and the more successful the post and result.

At the start of the first lockdown in March 2020, I began talking about growing your network and how powerful it can be. I felt this was relevant because, since last year, my network had increased by over 6,000 people, which have all been, bar a few, inbound connections.

I've given away a lot of free content and a lot of free value. People are thus more likely to spend time, whether on social media or the phone, engaging with me.

I've run competitions on social media posts, asking consultants if they want to win a copy of my book, Top Biller. If yes, they should tag three consultants in the comments and share the post. These methods have hugely helped to grow my network.

Over the last twelve months, I've pushed myself to do things, where I know there's an active audience, which has allowed me to get in front of a higher proportion of new people.

Last week I did a live Q&A with a recruitment agency. It was a 45-minute session whereby eighteen consultants could ask me questions. In the past, I might have refused, but these days I grab opportunities when they come by. All this activity, again, tracks back to Daniel Priestley's 'Key Person of Influence'. Whether I'm the key person of influence in construction recruitment, recruitment training, or the recruitment consultant that 'wrote the book', I'm constantly assessing how I can get to a larger audience in the quickest timeframe. I want to be in a position where I can say, 'I'm looking for a QS to start Monday', and my network helps me fill it as soon as possible. I don't choose where the answer is going to come from; I'm pretty happy for anybody and everybody to get involved and help.

Who stays and who goes?

I think the last twelve months have certainly softened competitiveness within the recruitment industry. The fact that I can create a Facebook group and have friendly collaboration is unusual. Many people enter the industry thinking they're going to make some quick money by putting some bums on seats and then go and buy flashy cars and watches. This can be true when the market's good, but the recent challenging market has humbled many in the industry. The ones looking for a quick buck have found the last year too tricky, and they've left. So, we have ended up with honest, hardworking, ethical recruiters that don't know any different but to build long lasting relationships.

If I think back to the recession in 2008, when I first set up a new region for a recruitment agency, it was a similar market; good recruiters survived because they added value and gave more back than they received. At one point, seventeen recruitment agencies were going out of business every week! That's a hell of a lot, but it was because they hadn't built strong enough relationships. You often have recruiters with only six months of experience who will set up their own recruitment business thinking it's easy. The moment the market gets a bit tougher, they realise their relationships with clients and candidates aren't robust enough to make it work.

A network is a giant web of relationships, which is why I always respond to people. I don't want to be the recruiter that sends a CV, and you never hear anything back. It happens all the time in this business; clients often speak to consultants and never hear a jot back. I always respond, whether it's a comment or a direct message on social media. It goes both ways – some people will put a post out there, and it will do well in terms of engagement, and yet they sit back and watch everyone else engaging with their posts and don't reply or engage themselves. This is not good practice and is where the ego can get in the way. You should try engaging with every single person that comes along, even if it's a slight nod of acknowledgement. Engagement drives engagement – give more than you take.

Before the Zuckerberg's of this world gave ordinary folk a social media platform, the only journeys that we could follow were of famous people in magazines and newspapers. We used to feel like we had a relationship with that celebrity, even though they were strangers. With social media, starting a personal brand now is easier than ever. We are appearing on people's timelines, and people can have a relationship with regular people like us! Responding to their engagement might even give them that a bit of rush, like if you were to see a famous person in public and get an autograph!

If you don't engage with those who make an effort, people might not bother again as they won't feel 'heard'.

Buying followers – yes or no?

A lot of people on social media buy followers, certainly on Instagram. So, you've got all these bots that will increase your followers and guarantee this, that, and the other, but in my opinion, there's little point in having a massive following if none of them engages or participates. You are better off having a smaller audience that engages in your content. That way, you will organically grow a network that's relevant and suitable. I think it's important to be a part of the community and engage with other people's content too. I don't sit for hours liking or commenting on posts, but there might be a ten-minute window when perhaps I'm on hold to the water board, and I spend some time spreading the love and engaging with other's content. It helps to build your network, and you're not just wasting time social media surfing.

Influential people

If you want to engage with influential people, you're better tagging them into a comment or responding to something they've posted than sending them a direct message. Remember, people with big followings often hire other people to answer their messages anyway, so even if you get a reply, it might not be them that's responding to you; it'll be their social media manager.

I first started to tag influential people by posting about the book I was reading that week. I'd find the author and tag them in my post, and would often get a thank you back from the author in the comments with a variance of the following;

'Thank you for the shout out.'

'I appreciate the post.'

'Glad you enjoyed it.'

Their engagement helps to elevate my brand simply by association.

Podcasts and interviews

On the back of the success of Top Biller, I decided to launch a podcast. My view is that if I can talk to powerful and influential people within and outside recruitment, it will complement the book and the journey.

Some people might listen to the podcast and not yet know I've written a book; and some might read the book and find the podcast. I can grab different people from different audiences depending on how they prefer to absorb content.

Last week I interviewed eight people for my podcast. I specifically pursued influential and motivational people with huge followings to speak. One of them was Greg Savage, who is a hugely successful recruiter in Australia. Greg's LinkedIn has over 300,000 followers, which makes my healthy following seem entirely insignificant. He also has a huge blog sign-up list of recruiters. He said that once the interview is published, he will reshare it on his LinkedIn. So that interview alone, in terms of growing my network, is priceless. It's leverage to the next level. Thanks Greg!

I've also spoken with Michaela Wain, who was a finalist on the BBC hit show The Apprentice, who has also been in construction for over eleven years. Again, when we finished the interview, she agreed to promote it to her 35,000 followers on Instagram, plus her 30,000 strong network on LinkedIn. It's a great opportunity.

Any opportunity to leverage your network with somebody else's should be taken. It benefits both parties and tells your audience that you are willing to grow and increase the quality of your added value.

Keep ahead of the curve

The market is constantly changing, and now you must have a reason to contact an individual – it's more sophisticated but also creates and adds better value. I used to sit on the sofa, create a targeted list of contacts and on a Friday night with a beer in hand, I just pressed 'connect' repeatedly on LinkedIn to build my network. I've since learnt that it is a waste of precious time and potential engagement. Better to put out content that's engaging, that attract people to you to connect as oppose to the other way round.

My Journal:

9th March 2020

Friday last week was a good day as we recorded the interview / podcast for Entrepreneur Truths with Kelly Forrester and Martin Miller. It was a really relaxed, informal chat which was actually enjoyable with challenging questions.

Also, last week I completed the interview for Talentwolf – a recruiter platform that at first sight seems more prevalent in Australia than here – but could be great exposure either way.

The Book marketing is still going strong, although stock piles are reducing for prize giveaways and influencer postings – new order likely to be needed – certainly with Austin, Texas coming up next month.

10th April 2020

Today I conducted my podcast interview with Dualta Doherty – a great chat to a genuinely open, honest and hardworking guy – well connected and very much motivated to be successful. Dualta has conducted numerous interviews and was very keen to chat to me and promote the book. I am looking forward to listening back and seeing what sort of response the podcast gets. Dualta was very kind in offering 6-7 names that I should be speaking to in order to boost my personal brand and further

> *gain some exposure. So that will be my task over the Easter weekend – to make contact and see where it leads.*
>
> ## 12ᵗʰ April 2020
>
> *Just a quick note entry (as it is a Saturday!) – Greg Savage who has a huge recruitment network and following down under put a post out today about Top Biller – and my contacts, network and messages went berserk – the comments and likes continued to grow throughout the weekend and was definitely worth the cost of sending him the book – a great post and if definitely sold a fantastic number of books – thanks Greg Savage – author of The Savage Truth – another great recruitment book.*

Remember, as I have discovered, we never know what opportunities a contact may have for us unless we connect with them. To network solely within your niche is potentially limiting your success. Go and meet people, tell them what you do, find out what they do, make genuine relationships. Good connections will end up benefiting you in the long run, and with a more extensive network, the more opportunity you will have to build them.

CHAPTER SEVEN

Adding Value

You can't build a reputation on what you are going to do.

— Henry Ford

Adding value allows you to build up trust and confidence with your audience and give your network more reasons to engage with you. This chapter will discuss how I have added value during my personal branding journey, how it has benefited my cause, and how you can do the same.

Adding value, from a personal branding perspective, is about giving more than you take. If you go out there to add value and change the direction of something, you create a bigger mission than you and attract a far wider audience. When I did the first set of strategy calls during the early stages of lockdown, a whopping 62 recruiters booked in on a global scale.

In the beginning, I wasn't thinking globally; I was thinking locally and small. However, the mission grew; the 62 people were from all over the world, making me think on a much grander scale.

From that point onwards, when I was doing my social media posts, my free webinars, creating and implementing the free strategy calls, it became a bigger journey and mission. I set out to appeal to the most significant pain points across the market. It didn't matter where they were sitting; whether they were in South Africa, Switzerland, Japan, or the UK, the problems or the pain points were the same. So, in terms of adding value and delivering, if you can find solutions to issues on a big scale, you add value to a greater audience.

The strategy calls were about personal branding and adapting to a changing landscape in a changing market and how to go about it. During the 30-minute Zoom calls, I offered solutions and ways in which individuals could implement strategies, tasks, and new ways of thinking and working. It started me on a journey of solving the global pain points with recruiters. It was the defining moment in terms of adding value on a much bigger scale than I'd first anticipated. Adding value means people will come to you time and time again because they know that they're going to learn something and potentially find that nugget of information that they can then implement.

Following my journey

I believe that simply allowing people to follow my journey has added value. When I post that I'm having a tough day, struggling this week, or even when I was admitted to hospital, it was scary showing signs of weakness and vulnerability. Still, it draws people in because, naturally, people are going through the same. Those people might not post about it but they feel empowered to comment on someone else's post. It makes it easier to share the problem.

Remember that commenting is still content. If all I ever did was comment on other people's posts and offer an opinion, add value, and communicate, it would still be relevant content. Don't forget that social media is a way to be social, it's not a one-way process. If you're going to put a post out and simply wait for people to comment and yet you don't engage back, it's not going to succeed. You must engage your audience by being social and using the comments to define the discussion further.

This is still true if the commentators make you uncomfortable and take the discussion in a different direction. Remember that everyone has a right to an opinion. You might disagree or agree, but adding value allows for healthy debate, even if you still sit on opposing sides.

There are things that I have done over the last twelve months that had no monetary value to me but have elevated my personal brand higher, so I have become recognised and noticed in other areas. Offering help, tips and tricks, potential strategies and ways of working are all methods of adding value. Even liking or interacting with the post without commenting is good. The fact that your name pops up adds tremendous value.

Ways I have added value in the last twelve months.

- Numerous free webinars, which are all over an hour-long, with a question-and-answer session and a free giveaway at the end
- Free 'business development challenge' in the Facebook group
- Free Facebook Group
- Podcasts interviews, both standalone and interviews, as the guest and host
- Live Q&A's with recruitment teams.
- Free 1-2-1 strategy calls
- Free handouts, tips, advice & support
- Free PDF documents on specific subjects

I've run many competitions giving my book away for free, specifically for consultants on furlough, and giveaways when the book hits certain milestones.

The main thing with adding value is you've got to think about your audience, who you're trying to attract with your personal branding and what messages you're trying to get out there.

Look at your audience's pain points – what can you do to help? It might be as simple as offering CV tips or interview tips or how to conduct yourself in a recruitment process – both from a client or candidate perspective, or how to make sure that you get chosen for those opportunities & stand out from the crowd. It might be that you talk to clients and companies about conducting a proper recruitment process, how to pre-qualify candidates before an interview, how to make sure the process runs smoothly and the benefits of interview-based questions, like PPA tests or psychometric testing.

There are many ways you can add value and open up a debate. There is no monetary gain, but you're showing a passion for the industry that you're in & looking to add value.

Most recruiters that post aren't adding value. They see platforms as another avenue to advertise their jobs, promote what they sell, from which they gain little impact because it's a pitch. If you're just posting vacancies, you're one dimensional. Whereas if you show your journey as well and the ups and downs, and how they affect you, you become three dimensional.

A lot of people don't believe that anybody would be interested in their journey.

"I'm nothing special. Why would anyone care if I'm having a good day or a bad day?"

But, it's not about that. If someone is having the same sort of day as you, they can feel like they're part of something else. And they can then get involved because you've allowed that release. As an industry, recruitment is filled with ego and loud and brash people that are pretty happy to shout from the hilltops when they win but don't often share how tough it can be when it doesn't work.

"I'm the best thing in the world. I'm the best recruiter, and you should always come to me because I am the one that will make the difference," they say.

This is recruitment – puffing your chest out to say, "I'm bigger and better than anyone else".

From a branding and a social media perspective, showing weakness or vulnerability might seem counter-intuitive, yet it allows people to come along on your journey, making you more approachable.

Vulnerability is not a weakness. The fact that you're willing to put it out there shows strength. I do it because I feel compelled to humanise those of us that work within recruitment.

The most engagement I have had on a post was when I spoke out about experiencing low points because of the pandemic. That post had an incredible amount of views and comments. It lifted my profile because it gave others a platform to vent their own distress. Showing vulnerability in our culture is another word for bravery.

Imagine a bunch of guys in a pub who are bantering. Then, one starts to talk about some problems he is having in his relationship; it opens the floodgates for the other guys to either offer help or talk about their relationship problems. It's creating a platform or a stage for people to open up.

People forget that social media is about being social and being honest. I quite often have a conversation with Tom in the office here.

"I don't know what to post today. What can I put out there?" he will say.

"Well, what's happened this week? How are you feeling today?" I ask

"I don't know. I feel a bit deflated because the client offered less than what the candidate wanted. And I was thinking that was going to be my first offer." He says.

"Well talk about that then – that's your content."

How you feel and how you deal with things from an emotional perspective will grab the most engagement and show that you are real. We, as recruiters, are rejected often and deal with many emotional things on a daily basis, whether that's someone else's emotions or our own. It is a rollercoaster journey, and sharing, educates the audience that recruitment is not an easy ride. If you can be honest and add value, you will engage your audience more organically.

If you are new to your industry and don't feel that you have much to offer, think again. Your journey is as valuable from day one as it is on day four thousand. There is always going to be one person a step behind you in the journey.

Believe in the whole journey – even the beginning and show the progress.

Maybe you've made your first placement or found your first client. You might've sold your first product if you work in a different industry. Show people that you're genuine, that you're trying to progress and doing everything you can to make things happen. If you consistently turn up, you will add value regardless.

You don't need to reinvent the wheel trying to create something that's nobody's ever done before. If you look at the most prolific social media people, what they post is nothing new. It might be a collection of thoughts; it might be something that's happening; it might be a quote. It might be questions that divide an audience and engage. The important part is consistency.

"I'm looking forward to the upcoming week, I have got lots of client calls booked in" is enough; it doesn't need to be heavily detailed. It doesn't need to be creative; it doesn't need to be new; it just needs to be you!

You can't make money from something you haven't done, and the longer you wait, the less likely you are to do it. Just do it. If you spend time perfecting; your productivity plummets. There is no such thing as perfect; it's another word for 'procrastinate'.

Collaboration within competition

Nobody has disrupted the recruitment market, and I want to be the one to do it, at least in terms of adding value from a personal brand and a social media perspective. It's all about innovation and collaboration and getting recruiters together to share ideas, processes, procedures and best practice. We can share 'hard to fill' vacancies. We can help candidates that other consultants are struggling to place.

There has been lots of healthy and honest debate within the Facebook group, and it's been hugely refreshing. You don't get many recruiters that will put their hand up and say, "I need help filling this position." Or "I can't find a place for this candidate. Can anyone else help?" My Facebook group is now doing just that. It's brought a market of competitors together to help. Day by day, it's slowly adding elements of disruption into what is at times a rather archaic industry. I'm adding value on the basis that I'm helping recruiters realise that it's not just about them, and as a collective group, we can fill more vacancies and become more successful. It's not just about that one position or one candidate; it's about collaboration within the competition— it's about the bigger picture.

When you've got to a point where you realise that your mission is bigger than everything else and far more significant than anything around you, you can start to change the face of everything. It becomes part of who you are.

If I can help people progress around me, then we all collectively get further forward in the journey. It is my management and leadership style; if I could get my consultants performing at their highest level and all doing well, we will all be happier. They enjoy being at work, which in turn means the office does well. The team does well. I do well, and everything's good. And at the same time, we all share the journey to a collective goal because we're all part of the same path, pushing towards the same goals.

Adding value is two-fold. Firstly, if somebody wants a position filling or they are looking for a new opportunity, and you're consistently on their timeline showing what you do, the first person that comes to mind is you.

But secondly, on a mindset level, adding value brings day-to-day contentedness, happiness, and satisfaction by doing things for other people. A serving mindset will increase your happiness levels in which will, in turn, increase your success. I think there's a lot to be said for just giving more than you take.

There was a lot of trial error in my efforts to add value that would be beneficial to my cause and valuable to my audience. If you feel that you have something that could be useful to your audience, offer it. It will increase your engagement, encourage growth and, crucially, give something back to your industry.

CHAPTER EIGHT

Journaling

Journaling has been incredibly valuable on this journey, as it has allowed me to reflect on my journey both in real-time and in hindsight. It's given me the opportunity for growth as once the ideas were down on paper, it made them tangible and thus achievable. Journaling can also reveal a lousy idea that seemed great in the brain but less so on paper.

I recommend anybody on any journey to journal their progress, as it helps us focus on our goals and gives us a more precise roadmap for our future success. To inspire you and prove that a journal does not need to read like Shakespeare (and illustrate that a personal branding journey can include many necessary highs and lows) I have included my musings for you to enjoy.

My Journal

2nd May 2020

What a rollercoaster of a week – it's been a MASSIVELY REWARDING week and easily one of the busiest since the lockdown began back in March.

On Friday 24th April, I put a post out on LinkedIn, saying I was opening my diary for the whole of this week and any consultants/recruitment businesses that need a 1-2-1 chat can contact me. The post read:

"If you are at a low ebb, feeling demotivated, overwhelmed, frustrated, anxious, concerned or just want to share some innovative ideas, ambitions or motivations, then I am here to chat."

I did this as I wanted to offer some VALUE back to the market.

To be honest, I thought I would have 10-12 calls booked in across the course of the week, but to my surprise & delight ended up being 10-15 calls per day.

62x 30minute Zoom calls later, I had spoken with consultants and businesses worldwide, including Switzerland, Japan, Singapore, South Africa, the US, Australia, New Zealand, Ireland, Canada and the UK.

The calls created so much VALUE and CONTENT. ALL calls were recorded and packed with valuable content, ideas, suggestions, and challenges. It was fascinating talking to so many individuals from a variety of backgrounds.

The common theme amongst the week was either 'what do I do whilst I am on furlough?" and "how do I stay relevant and present and ensure my clients remember me when I go back to the office?". Every area of recruitment was covered; from consultants looking to start up their own business to building a new desk, managing their current desk and looking for support in where they currently are. The plan is to write up all of the notes from these conversations and give them back to the market, which will only offer more content and value to individuals who want to read.

I also managed to get six potential new clients – businesses – looking for help on the mentoring, coaching and recruitment support, something I need to work on in readiness for the end of next week.

I recorded my podcast interview with Hishem Azzouz – what a nice guy. Great interview, relaxed and informal discussing my journey and my plan moving forward.

I completed my first LIVE stream interview this week, too – talking to the lovely Catherine Byers Breet based over in Minneapolis in the US – a 30-minute live stream – which went so fast. We discussed the Five Key Areas that Recruiters can and should act on to advance and make a difference. I believe it went well – the next area of self-development ticked off the list.

I had a good chat with Chris Taylor this week from Instagrammatics – asked him to help me build a sales funnel, build a process to engage, attract an audience, push the book, sales techniques, and coach into the forefront of what I do. I will also need to utilise social media to make an impact on the development and introduction of the APP (which is now signed off and LIVE! – but has no content of any note).

Lockdown / COVID-19

So, we are currently working towards the final week of the 2nd block of a three-week full lockdown. It's starting to get more difficult – the novelty has begun to wear off, and everyone is beginning to become a little more on edge. Our two boys, whilst they have been brilliant throughout, have started to get a little naughtier and push the boundaries of normal behaviour. I think they miss the change in company and activity (which we all do). It's getting a little like Groundhog Day.

The days are all the same; we try and change it up, do something different, keep the conversations varied, but ultimately nothing is happening. There is no sport, no live TV, no other news across the globe that isn't COVID-19 related – the updates are all about our ability to start moving more freely again – it's such a surreal world we are living in. We are reliant on the information we are given from the news, documentaries or reruns.

Currently, we are running at 26,000 UK deaths – which is a drastically high number (I think the initial discussions the UK were working towards 20,000 being a good number to be happy with!). Government and press and manipulation – who knows.

27th May 2020

So I haven't written much or journaled much over the last 2 – 3 weeks, which is a shame as I am sure I have missed a few of the ups and downs during that time. It's been a gruelling yet rewarding few weeks. I decided to embark on the journey with Chris Taylor to help me build sales funnels and help grow my book sales initially – this is the start of the funnel. I then wanted people to progress onto an online training programme that individuals could join, pay for and develop their own set of recruitment skills.

We decided on a 12-week programme from start to finish and to add as much value as possible. I wanted to create a one-stop-shop for recruiters to come and learn their trade and be fully trained, ready to be an excellent top performing consultant at the end of it. I appreciate that most salespeople and most recruiters stick their chests out and think – I don't need any training! So, I need to make sure that this is the best for detail as possible. I also felt it is essential to deliver a training package whilst I was still actively recruiting – this is important as I think most trainers and coaching out there is conducted by individuals that haven't recruited since the mid-90s, and things have drastically changed since then.

The idea is that there needs to be a core basis of videos/online training that takes you through the normal education of a recruiter – the basics of 12 core modules that form the "12 weeks Online Recruitment Mastery Programme":

- Laying the Foundation
- The Recruitment Process
- Structure
- The Client
- The Candidate
- The Vacancy
- The Interview
- The Offer and Placement
- Negotiation
- Online
- KPIs, Ratios and Stats
- Mindset, Motivation and Rejection
- PLUS, lots of Online Course Bonuses

So, for the last three weeks, I have worked my absolute arse off trying to collate all of the detail into a succinct programme. As of today, I have completed four modules in the hope I can get a couple more completed today and be halfway through.

Wrongfully, I assumed that as Top Biller had been compiled and wrote along similar lines, I had already written most of the content and just needed to add to video format. I was wrong. I missed so much in the way of content from Top Biller, not only does it make me feel that I need to write the 2nd edition after I have written the course content, but that there is an unbelievable amount of work that still needs to be done. My fear of failure or ridicule still rears its ugly head every so often. I want this course to be such good value that consultants are willing to pay more for it than I charge. I want them to go away knowing that they have improved as a consultant, obtained valuable information along the way and have received unbelievable content and value. The amount of additional online bonuses I include in the programme is growing daily and is hugely valuable.

Everything about this course build has to be relevant, UpToDate content that remains valid, and can be used in everyday recruitment life. I want each module to impact and offer something that the general recruiter doesn't already have. Each week I will be delivering a weekly one-hour live Zoom call/webinar where I will be free to take questions from the recruiters. These will be recorded and reposted into the training – so people can further develop from people that have gone before them.

The general course of each day is that I get up at 7 am and have a quick breakfast and coffee with the family and then travel across to the office. I have eight static whiteboards on my wall with bubble diagrams of each module, which include what I feel needs to be incorporated into each group, like facts, thoughts, tips and ideas that can help you advance. I pick a module to work on and then write up the content and use the book chapters too. I try and add as much as possible as I don't want feedback that the course is just my book regurgitated! This will leave people feeling shorted, and that they have overpaid for something that they could have got off Amazon for £12.99. So, the content takes about a day to write through, separated into various topics within each module.

Once I have the content written up, and I feel I have covered everything needed, I advance to a PowerPoint presentation where I try and make the slides as descriptive as possible, whilst still allowing me to talk through the points on the video. Once I am happy with the PowerPoint slide information, I work through and add stock photos, videos and some basic animation to the slides to try and make them a little more entertaining.

Once the slides are completed, I set up a Zoom meeting for each subject or topic within the module. So far, each module has had five topic areas. Each Zoom meeting is a recording where I film me talking through each set of PowerPoint presentations. The format is consistent throughout – part of me wonders whether the format will get a little tedious by the 4th, 5th, 6th week. Then, I must consider recording in huge daily blocks of video – some videos reaching an hour long! Recording them makes me get fed up with my own voice, however, the way the programme is set up is that the videos or modules will be released in stages. People can watch, pause, stop and repeat videos, so hopefully won't be sitting there losing the will to live as I continue to chat through my lessons.

There are parts of the course that get me excited, and I know instantly that there are parts that will add instant value – which is fantastic. The other pieces, where I am going through what seems obvious to me, is quite challenging. I have to keep reminding myself that there are recruiters out there that have little to zero training, and what may seem obvious to me isn't that obvious to them. All the little titbits of information and advice that comes through a simple sentence are worth their value. Fourteen years of experience crammed into a 12-week programme and written over four weeks' worth of long days in the office has to be good value, right? We will see.

The days are long, laborious, and about the process. It's a constant drive to get to the end of the programme to start monetising the information and create an income for my family from this day forward. The COVID-19 pandemic has taught me that if the world stops, global economies drop, and the countries across the world press pause – we need to have built a business that can at least survive if not prosper. My book sales have done exceptionally well, having now sold across 35 countries and continues to hit the Amazon no.1 spot. I believe it has been helped by the world being stationary. A considerable proportion of the recruitment industry seems to be on furlough and sat at home. Some choosing to enjoy the hot weather and the family home time; others are looking to advance and make a name for themselves by self-education and improving their potential for when they return to work, which is a great mindset to have. I am pushing to get the course out there before everyone returns to work. I have established some great connections worldwide via social media platforms of LinkedIn and Instagram mainly. I have made Zoom calls in Japan, Canada, Australia, New Zealand, Singapore, Ireland, the US and so on, which has enabled me to establish a global personal brand that is phenomenal and potentially huge as I look to grow my business.

I need to stop the nagging doubt that appears every so often, though – what if it all fails? What happens if it all goes wrong and I get ridiculed? I am not sure this will ever go away, and in many ways, it's what keeps me true to the cause. I don't want to be in a position where anyone ever says "that was crap" or "I didn't find any value in the content whatsoever", but when dealing with salespeople and recruitment consultants I suppose I always run that risk.

There is an important point I have come to realise during lockdown. When you work from home and your children are there because the schools are closed, they don't understand that you are at work. You being at home means they require your attention. They need you, and you are at home. It's unfair to be rude because of their interruptions – they just want to be involved, and it's tough to manage. Hence the move to the office – no interruptions, no distractions. The thought of missing out on their home time is challenging, and each day can be difficult to get through as you want to spend this time with them. COVID-19 has allowed the world to pause and take a breath, but the trouble is as both Emma and I are self-employed – we don't get paid unless we work. Hence the journey continues.

Comments and messages via social media continue to increase, and the momentum of conversations are coming via various sources now. It could be directly through email, LinkedIn predominantly, and consultants asking for a copy of the planner or recommended reading list. This has to be one of the better marketing ideas I have ever had, as I get an email address for every request. I also know from their request that they may struggle with structure and accountability, leading to a potential mentoring option.

So, I started in the office at 07.30 am this morning when I first typed today's words, it's now 10.06 pm, and I am sat in the kitchen typing still, waiting for the edits from today's video – 'Module 5 – The Candidate' – to upload and be sent across for final submission. I am so tired, but the sheer determination to provide for me and my family keeps me going.

Emma, Ethan, Hugo and Coco all went to the park today, and spent some time walking in the park, playing in the sun, and enjoyed an ice cream before returning home to sit in the front garden and have a picnic. A lovely day, and I am pleased that they can do that, but at the same time frustrated that I miss out. It's not their fault or anyone else's – it's my pure determination to spend the hours now working to create future freedom than to enjoy the freedom now. (Do you have what it takes to generate freedom Steve?? Or do you wait to be bailed out or offered a helping hand?) It's not for the faint-hearted, I tell you that much.

1st June 2020

Oh, my days, it's 1st June – we are already halfway through 2020 – where does the time go? What's crazier this year is that we have been in lockdown since the end of March – so a quarter of 2020 has been in isolation, less of a rush, schools, pubs, restaurant, businesses have all been closed and yet the time still shoots past – crazy!

So today is the official 1st day of the online 12-week recruitment mastery programme launch – working to a two-week build-up across all social media platforms and building a marketing presence for the big day.

The Launch of The Recruitment Mastery Programme

So, back to the 1st day of the launch, and today was all about The Reason WHY?! Why have I decided to create an online training course? What's my story? Why is recruitment training not as good as it should be during lockdown? What has been the one area or areas that I have been questioned about? Since I launched my book, I have been inundated with people with recruitment problems, questions and queries. This is my opportunity to answer those and start helping as many people as possible. So I dipped a few comments saying that I was working on a project in the background that will help solve all of those issues. I have thrown everything into the last four weeks, working every hour under the sun to create as much value and content as possible. The recruitment training market needs to be disrupted as its full of recruitment trainers from the 1990s who aren't relevant in today's market. This is the direction I am heading – who is with me? I asked people to COMMENT "I'm in" if they were interested. Across all media platforms on the 1st day, I captured the attention of about 20 recruiters – so 2/3 of the first intake there – should everyone be willing to pay! We will see.

2nd June 2020

2nd day of the 2-week programme launch today – very happy with yesterday's feedback and engagement and pleased that it didn't 'flop'. Now is the time to keep building the momentum and publicity as we work through each day.

So, today's post is all about 'What's the one thing that's held you back?' – common conversations with recruiters over the last few weeks have been centred around two areas:

- Lack of Structure and issues managing and valuing time.
- Lack of training.

These are the two most significant pain point areas as far as my conversations have revealed. I would be interested to know what you feel has held you back? My story is being held back at the start by overzealous KPIs and countless areas of justification, to the point where I felt suffocated by the 'box ticking' exercises I had to go through. The opportunity to move roles couldn't have come at a better time as it allowed me to take the KPIs, the stats and ratios that were important and generated a better level of return. Still, it allowed me to discard the rest and concentrate on growth and personal development, leading me to where I am today. Let's see what this post brings in and generates.

Hopefully, the momentum is starting to build, and the platforms I am building around me will stand the test of time and will continue to add value and earn us cash – even when we don't work. These last few weeks have been relentless as I can't switch off and think about anything else. Everything is about content, adding value, fulfilling the needs of the masses and helping as many people as possible. Despite all of this, all of the hours and time I have spent collating and writing up the training, I still have days of doubt, worry and stress. I don't want to be in a position of ridicule or critique. Whilst I know that will happen, I don't want it to, and this is the part that keeps me up at night!

3rd June 2020

Day three of the product launch was about sharing a short video, so I chose a short clip about Marginal Gains. I also took half a day today after collecting Hugo from school. It's been a trying week, and I was starting to feel the effects of too much work, too many late nights grafting and the mere stress of putting this together and worrying that it might not work. The element of doubt now as I am reaching the finish line is still apparent – and it's a strange one. The same happened with the book, so I see it as a positive because it will ensure that there is quality and value throughout the course. The last thing I want is to have someone not happy with the value or the content – so I will keep on grafting. A good solid rest and sleep and some time with the family will hopefully energise and get me back roaring to go again.

4th June 2020

So, feeling refreshed and ready to go.

This week is all about positioning knowledge – so one more video in the format of yesterday's (marginal gain video) and then Friday is about my story – 'my reason as to why I've dedicated time to build the training course'.

Sunday is about announcing and launching the product in a post at the lowest price I will ever sell it – but its application only.

Monday and Tuesday is more about value content and a call to action to apply before the price increases.

Wednesday evening, I will announce I am running a webinar the following Wednesday to give free training.

At this point, this is where the serious work will kick in.

Over the next two weeks, we will have built:

- the product sales page.
- the order form.
- the webinar landing page.
- application page.
- and email sequence confirming the product.

The first programme will need an agreed start date with the delegates, and the launch will go LIVE each morning over 12 weeks, and I will do a LIVE on Mondays and Thursdays to deliver group Q&A and training sessions.

It's all very exciting and nerve-racking at the same time – I feel sick with hope and trust that people will see value in working with me and learning as we move. I am confident I can add value moving forward and help consultants perform better. The documentation of the journey and continually pushing myself outside of my self-limiting beliefs is scary and motivating at the same time. I can't believe how much my life has changed since the end of March when lockdown began. I had never thought I would be able to shift paths so quickly and on the basis to help build a more consistent income for my family and me and add value to a larger audience – this could be the game changer!

On a completely separate note, I haven't forgotten the day job. The construction market is extremely slow – clients are cautious, sites aren't back to full working situations. Generally, staffing seems to be around 60% capacity as far as I can tell – clients certainly aren't looking for additional perm staff. I am getting zero response from any marketing. On the flip side, I do have a number of candidates daily, calling saying they are now looking for work, insecure about the job or advising they have been made redundant – it's a sad and challenging time in construction. There are a lot of worried people out there.

I just added up my book sales for May as the notifications come through:

Total profit for May is a whopping £1,179.24!!

Since it was published in November, that's my first 4 figure month – feeling ecstatic about that, selling 61 copies in GERMANY alone!

5ᵗʰ June 2020

It's Friday – the weather is horrible, rain streaming down the windows and everywhere is grey and drab, not your most motivating welcome to the day, but hey, I think in some ways it's easier to work on days like this than the days when the sun is shining through. All you want to do on those days is run in the park with your family.

So, yesterday's posts went well on social media, despite the issues with the mic on my phone – the sound quality was dreadful, but the content was well received. The new phone has arrived, so I have fixed that problem now (hopefully!)

I took a few calls yesterday from individuals looking for work. I sense that frustration and hostility are increasing as people start to worry about what the future holds. The markets are uncertain, the economy, whilst it would appear, is recovering, and indexes and stocks are on the rise – on the ground at the forefront tells a different story; it's very surreal and a little odd. More and more candidates finding themselves out of work, furloughed still, or redundant, businesses starting to disappear, and the whole scenario seems to be getting a little darker. The levels of hospital admissions yesterday were nearly double the figures going back to 25th May – people are starting to get more and more relaxed in their social lives and general mixing – which isn't great. I believe the general population is just getting a little frustrated and taking liberties or their days into their own hands, with meet ups, parties, and gatherings etc.

So, todays task for the launch, day five, is all about me, my story and my why. 'Why have I decided to create and build an online training course – what's my motivator?' The big picture here is that I wanted to produce something of value back to the recruitment market whilst I am still actively recruiting – it's relevant, relatable, current. I believe it will add value to recruitment consultants' career and journey. The recruitment market lacks good quality, accessible training for the individual – those who are motivated, ambitious, driven and keen to self-educate. I want to work with consultants committed to the journey, committed to learning and aiming for higher levels of achievement. I have a lot of experience and value that people can learn from and benefit from, and I think it's important to share this with as many individuals looking to develop as possible. This is my duty and my cause back to the market. The programme will be on an application-only basis, and I will decide if the course is right for them or not. It's exciting stuff, and I believe it's my calling – after conducting all of those Zoom *calls during April, it showed me that the lack of training was evident, and there was a gap in the market to add real value. The majority of recruitment trainers in the market may well be very good trainers and deliver excellent results. Still, they haven't recruited for years, and I believe consultants see this and are less bought into the tactics and advice.*

I am recording the initial welcome video for the sales funnel and putting the content together to get things moving.

It goes something like this:

"Hey everyone, Steve Guest here. Thank you very much for declaring interest in the Recruitment Mastery Programme. I thought I'd do a quick video to talk you through how this all works.

Firstly, it's a 12-week programme that I have created that has the perfect blend of education and accountability. I've built this programme out of frustration in the industry with the fact everyone pours out information but never actually shows you how to do each thing step by step. My mission is to change the game, and this programme I hope you'll agree does that!

We cover everything from getting started to prospecting through to systems and scaling – for those of you that know me, you know I'm always one for the detail, so when I say it includes everything – I mean it.

The programme is application only, as I only want to work with people that are serious about taking action right now. So please, if this sounds like you, then scroll down, take a read of the programme information, investment and complete your application.

I look forward to speaking with you".

7th June 2020

It's a Sunday, and I am sat in the office, again, nice and early as its LAUNCH Day! Today is the day I get to tell the world via social media video that I am launching the Recruitment Mastery Programme. Scary stuff, buoyed by the energy and motivation to get the content out there and energised for today to see what the response will be.

The video is very basic; simply explaining what the programme is all about and its application ONLY – I only want to work with the motivated and the ambitious. Delegates will be chosen by phone call and selected on merit—exciting and targeted stuff.

Video went out about 11.30 am, and I waited and waited. Then the messages and engagement started to happen – LinkedIn went crazy! I did cheat a little and added the links into all the 'group' WhatsApp's and asked everyone to get involved and share the support – which they duly did! Social media went nuts until about 4 pm and then quietened but carried on throughout the day. Let's just hope we get a few sign ups now, and we can start building some income and revenue.

8th June 2020

Social Media continues to gain momentum, and the 'YES' comments continue through. I haven't looked at who and how many have followed through and signed up, but it's a start. Still, plenty of time to push for my interested parties this week and next, so we will see. The initial target is 30, and I believe I am somewhat away from that, thinking more like five at present.

At breakfast this morning, I had the first moment of real doubt creep in again – the worry that people won't find value, or think that the training isn't good– which obviously I don't want and am doing everything in my power to avoid. Like anything, my style won't suit all, and not everyone responds in the same way. Just take the book reviews for example – vast amounts of 5* reviews but that doesn't stop the 1* and 2* reviews. People will always have an opinion and not frightened of putting it out there. Nerves are a good thing – don't get me wrong – they ensure that I add even more value, but it does affect your mindset in fleeting moments.

Today is Launch Day eight, and I will be sharing another video of value at some point today – which hopefully will be well received again and add further value to the programme.

I've announced the competition winners on LinkedIn today. Ten Audiobook winners and twelve Paperback winners – which has already gone crazy on comments and likes etc. It's all well planned to create momentum and get consultants looking at my profile and hopefully join the programme. I need to be more confident in my ability and push the link everywhere.

I will be shipping copies of my book to South Africa, Australia, New Zealand, Ireland and the UK; it's an expensive piece of marketing, but if I get one person signed up from this list, it will be worth it!

9th June 2020

Today I feel deflated. After all of the hard work, the hours, the stress, the early mornings and late nights and yet I know I need to up the ante – stop feeling sorry for myself and make things happen! Just having a moment of weakness on a Tuesday – sometimes it's good to let it raise its ugly head just to give you the kick up the backside that you need! Stop whining and make it happen. Moments like this just remind me of the quote from the film The Rock – one of my all-time favourite films.

John Patrick Mason: Are you sure you're ready for this?
Stanley Goodspeed: I'll do my best
John Patrick Mason: Your "best"! Losers always whine about their best. Winners go home and f**k the prom queen.
Stanley Goodspeed: Carla was the prom queen!
John Patrick Mason: Really?
Stanley Goodspeed: [cocks his gun] Yeah.

Day nine of the launch today, too, so another day of video content. I think today is going to be about the combination of office and work-based work and the ability to know and understand what's being done and what's not; motivation to hit targets and overachieve, certainly in a sales environment, and what motivates you to hit higher levels of achievement. One hundred calls in a week, and you can have Friday off? Would you do it?

Today's content creation is all about ONLINE – a topical subject that elevates you to a higher level.

10th June 2020

Another day another dollar.

Feeling a little better today; I had an entire day of feeling sorry for myself yesterday. I perhaps didn't quite appreciate that it would be an arduous journey to get those first few people involved and ready for the journey. The first delegates will be the hardest as we have to get them onboard, service the need, match their levels of expectation and offer a return in value.

Day ten – Launch – Today! I am announcing a webinar for next Wednesday. I am looking to offer three secrets that enable me to stand out from everyone else, and what I do that allows me to perform at a higher level? This has got to have some serious thought to it. My initial thoughts are:

PERSONAL BRAND *– as a Recruiter, what can you do that will elevate your Personal Brand to a higher level.*

POSITIONING *– as a Recruiter, how can you position yourself in your market as the 'go-to' individual or 'key person of influence.'*

MARGINAL GAINS *– how can you implement Marginal Gains across your daily routine that will ensure you improve your return*

STRUCTURE *– How can you change your daily structure to improve your output?*

The post did well, and the feedback in regards to the webinar has been strong. The date has been set for Thursday 18th June 2020 at 4 pm (it was meant to be Wednesday, but Aston Villa are LIVE on TV for their first game back during / post lockdown, and I know my concentration would waiver!), so we will see. Still pushing to deliver and put myself out of my comfort zone – I have never delivered a training webinar before. It's a little bit nerve-wracking, so fingers crossed.

11th June 2020

A day of home-schooling and working today – it's going to be eventful. The morning has started with the 3 X table, French food and money and maths, whilst working through all of the contacts that have shown an interest in the Mastery Programme. It's been a fun-packed start to the day! 😌

The plan for today is to focus on a particular area of the webinar and start suggesting ways that I have used it to position myself and my brand to create a market or business for me. So today is about picking a core subject from the four above, saying what it is, and how it has worked for me and elevated me to a higher level or made such an impact. The webinar topic will be about this: 'what areas within this topic would you like to discuss in further detail?'

It's been a little distracting today.

The choice is Personal Brand and Positioning – what have I done to elevate my brand to higher levels, and what has it allowed me to achieve? My network on LinkedIn has now grown to 26,000 connections and mostly organic connections.

We will cover everything from a professional profile photo, professional purpose, optimising your LinkedIn profile, differentiating from the competitors, defining your professional purpose, articulate your experience and how to value your *target audience. Social media has allowed professionals a magnificent opportunity to become more discoverable, sharable and memorable through their personal brand.*

Personal Brand allows you to establish credibility, grow your network, increase your marketing, attract new opportunities, increase sales, position, educate, and inspire.

Personal Branding allows you to show the world your journey, the ups and downs, the highs, and the lows; you get to show your motivations, core values, ethics, and your business strengths. You get to promote who you are and what you stand for in a non-salesy way.

People struggle with wanting the immediate payoff, and when they don't see the £ signs, they stop – that leaves a perfect opportunity for the rest of us. Social media and personal branding requires persistence and the requirement to add into your everyday working life.

Personal Brand allows you to show your individuality – which in essence is the core of any recruiters' journey. What makes you any different to all of the other recruiters I speak to – the answer was always "me". Personal Brand is the perfect opportunity to expand on this and truly show who you are. It is the 'differentiator'.

The videos '10 in 10 Challenge' – what an eye-opener that was. The exposure this gained and was all types of contacts, new, old, distant and forgotten. The clients discussed me with consultants who went on visits. I was getting communication from the market with suggestions of what to do and what to say.

The idea of having a strategy behind your personal branding and your process of posting – I try and work to a 70 / 20 / 10 rule in that I post 70% about my business, the market and what I specialise in – this is the core of element of my brand. 20% is about me as an individual, so what I do, how I work, what is personal to me, what motivates me, and inspires and empowers me to grow. 10% is what is trending – so picking something that is in the news that is gaining engagement and traction – be careful with this as you want to divide opinion but stay true and loyal to your core values.

15th June 2020

Day 14 of Launch – so it's Monday again, back in the office nice and early, coffee, a bottle of water and toast in tin foil all set to go! Feeling refreshed today and raring to go.

This is the week I also conduct my first 'LIVE' online webinar – something I haven't ever done before, and by the looks of things, there could be a whole host of people involved and tuning in – could be huge game-changer – let's hope I don't embarrass myself and it all goes to pot! The webinar is all about PERSONAL BRAND, so it should be enough to talk about for one hour, with questions and the sell at the end – or OFFER! I have high hopes for this week and would like to think that we will get some sign-ups – if people can find the cash!

The webinar format will be a collection of my best-kept secrets and will be documented as my key THREE SECRETS from your PERSONAL BRAND:

- The element to your business that will 10X your performance when implemented effectively.

- *How you can create a lead generation machine that never sleeps.*
- *How to get your market to work for you – improving speed, efficiency, engagement whilst building your network further.*

Over the last few weeks, I have learnt and effectively grown my experience across various platforms, including Powerpoint, Zoom, Calendly, Typeform, Go To Webinar, and continually looking to add to my experience to improve customer journeys and appreciation. I have uploaded my Top Biller audiobook to the Findaways platform and created accounts to enable the opportunity to grow my potential revenue and network. This is all part of the long game and imperative to add to my personal growth journey. It's continuous, arduous and scary!

Yesterday was all about the LINK going LIVE for the webinar. I systematically went through everyone who had said YES or I'M IN on my last few posts and sent them the link to register. Later on yesterday evening, I went through every LinkedIn message I had received about Top Biller and privately messaged them the link and suggested the sign-up. When I had left the office, I was on 22 registered sign-ups for the webinar – Chris, my social media strategy guy, gave me a target of 50 registrations! My response was simple and straightforward – I have spent the last 14 years doubling any target I had been given – 100 is the aim. If I can find over this number and hopefully get 100 people involved, I will be a happy man.

16th June 2020

Today I walked into the office early (it's 7.30 am) as I had a call scheduled for 8 am with a potential client for the programme and wanted a chat about construction and recruitment; this was cancelled due to a burst pipe in the roof of his house. So, it allowed me to write a bit more here and check in on the sign-ups, drum roll, please; 86 sign-ups and registrations! Very pleased with that!

18th June 2020 –The First EVER LIVE Webinar

It has been crazy the last few days, which is why I haven't written much here – the webinar has been off the scale. The latest count was 152 registrations for a webinar that holds just 100 people – oversubscribed within 24 hours – which is just insane! This is my first ever webinar – and it's LIVE, and I have now got to make sure that I deliver VALUE to every single individual that stays the course of the webinar. I feel sick, nervous, anxious, excited and motivated. I have woke up today, in the zone, and ready to go – the downside is that I need to wait out another 10 hours until I get started. This is the tricky bit for me now – I just want to get it done and dusted so I can relax again.

My biggest worry and frustration, which is crazy, isn't the content or my ability to talk through the slides – it's the fact that the webinar is on 'go to webinar' – a platform I haven't used before. It gives me palpitations and pushes my anxiety levels up a few notches – even writing this now, I can feel the blood pulsating and my focus shifting. It's a state of mind that I need to learn to manage – I know it will be fine once I get going and I pray that there are no technical issues because that will really scupper me.

There are 67 slides of what I see as true value – lots of valuable content that will enable people to leave the webinar and have actionable steps to put in place to improve their personal brand – what I also have to portray is that this presentation is one chapter out of 72, and so the value you can get from this is massive.

It's 2.19 pm, and in 1hr and 40 minutes until I go LIVE in front of 100 recruitment consultants and recruitment business owners to offer my VALUE and CONTENT. To say I am starting to get nervous would be an understatement – the importance of pushing your limits and putting yourself into situations that scare you is insane! The realisation of what I do every week to feel uncomfortable does give me fleeting moments of weakness.

2.53 pm – Sweaty palms, heavy head – this shit is real! I am so looking forward to getting to the end of the webinar already so that I can breathe a big sigh of relief and check off another milestone! Let's hope the feedback is good!

I did a runner! I legged it to the petrol station for a cappuccino and a bar of chocolate – hopefully, that settles the pre-webinar jitters! It's crazy how apprehensive I get over the tiny things; what happens if I forget how to share my screen! What happens if this happens and that happens. Oh, to live in my head!

I am ready to go!

It's pretty funny; I sit here, awaiting the run-up to 4 pm, nerves jangling, heart rate pulsing, head starting to ache on the anticipation of achieving something that scares me and is out of my comfort zone. It's not that the content doesn't have value, not at all, I know the content and value is there – it's the worry of something new, something I haven't done before and the nervousness of a technical hitch or forgetting to do something.

I log in at 3.55 pm – just to break the ice, if nothing more, say hello, check the sound and the visual. 40+ people are already logged in and ready to go – I dip in with a 'hi, this is Steve, just checking in to see that everything works, can you all hear me, comment YES in the chatbox – can everyone see me?' The YES's start to roll in. Great news – we will be ready to start in about 60 seconds or so. I mute and hide my screens again, take a sip of water, deep breath, stand up and prepare myself. The ice is broken! I am as ready as I will ever be. I log back in and commence my intro:

"Thank you to everyone for joining me today – I have had over 150 people register for my first ever webinar! For a limit of 100 people – which is simply amazing – all of you who have managed to get in – hats off to you for arriving early and getting here! I have always championed the 'early arrivers', so it kind of fits with my character!

I am on a mission to change and disrupt the recruitment market forever – I want to change the way it functions, how we, as recruiters, are trained, coached and mentored and above to improve all of our potential returns, sales and billings. I believe the recruitment market has been waiting for disruption for a long time!

So, for today: -

How many of you here understand the importance of PERSONAL BRAND and DIFFERENTIATING within your market – let me know with a YES in the comments.

The important part here is that YOU as an individual need to start being accountable, being creative, being entrepreneurial in your thought process to make it happen alongside your regular daily routine, activity, targets and KPIs.

The reason I decided to do this webinar today is for the very reason that for everyone that commented YES in the comments box. Suppose I can help you get your message across, your service out to more people. In that case, we can collectively and proactively change the face of recruitment – improve the reputation the understanding and help remove the constant negativity that we face every day.

I am genuinely excited to share my ideas and journey with you.

So, for the purposes of today, I want to show you:

How you can instantly start differentiating YOU with your marketing and sales techniques to enable you to stand out in your market and outmanoeuvre your competitors.

Is everyone ok with that? Give me a YES in the comments.

So, if I share a tiny part of my journey with you, I honestly believe that there is not a single person in this webinar that I can't help, coach and mentor to achieve higher levels of improvement within the next 12 months of their recruitment journey. I firmly believe that you could be new to recruitment or have been in the industry longer than me; I can add value and improve the way you work to bring new levels of billings. I want you all to believe in this as strongly as I do.

I am a seasoned Recruiter; I have an obsession to help recruiters, recruitment businesses and consultants to perform at higher levels. I have been mentored and coached by some fantastic people out there in the market place. Now I will continue to improve, advance on this journey.

I want to change the world of recruitment and disrupt the traditional way of recruiting and coaching and enhance the changes in the market to make better recruiters!"

19th June 2020

What a success!

My first ever LIVE webinar went really well and I am so happy with the results.

- 152 register.
- 88 turned up.
- 64 remained to the end.
- Forty were still there for questions.

All of the nerves and worries leading up to it were worth it – it allowed me to care and ensure there was enough value in the webinar. It lasted about two hours and was really well received; lots of people completed their first videos today, too and tagged me in, so LinkedIn has gone a little crazy, to say the least. Let's see how many people follow through and do their ten videos in ten days. So, the next webinar will be a week on Wednesday – looking to choose a topic of value again – I personally think Structure because so many people lack discipline in sales, and it's where you can make the most difference.

My heart and head are still racing from the webinar. Amazingly, I have gone from being relatively unknown six months ago in the recruitment world to conducting my first webinar and talking/

If you have a voice or an opinion and do things to change for the better, the more powerful and more global you can differentiate on and solve the masses' problems. The greater the brand, the greater the audience and the network you will receive. I believe it's about having a mission that is bigger and more powerful than your day-to-day duties. I created the Recruitment Mastery Program to add value on a much larger scale and create something that was accessible and differentiated me from a lot of other trainers or coaches. It just so happened that the COVID-19 pandemic's timing and everything around it helped develop my mission because everything was suddenly all virtual and online. I spotted the opportunity, overcame the hurdles, and it has served me wonderfully so far.

I have no hidden agenda or preconceived plan of where it all might end up. I'm just going through the journey, and if things pop up along the way, I will either go at them full throttle or dismiss them and carry on.

Differentiation is the ability to position yourself where you feel fit, find pain points in your industry and deliver on them.

As part of the recruitment mastery program, we conducted a live Zoom group discussion. The conversation topic was how to be more consultative as opposed to being your average, typical recruiter. The point behind it was to get recruitment consultants to add vast amounts of value to their network, supply chain, and clients and candidates by going over and above the expectation. A recruiter expects to register a vacancy, go and match it with some CV's, and send the candidates across for the clients to interview. Then you negotiate the process, and hopefully, we have a happy outcome and a well-placed candidate. That's what every recruiter should be doing. The ability to promote who you are as an individual and to harness and differentiate you as a consultative person adds value to the supply chain.

So how do you do that? Do you pick up on a previous life experience? Sure, you can use where you have previously worked, what you've trained in, what skill sets you've got, what you've educated yourself through, what degree you have, and what life skills you have that can add value either in your market, your sector, or your specialism. For example, before I first started recruiting, I was specialising in managing e-Auctions towards the end of my career as a buyer – an e-auction for those that don't know, from a procurement aspect was to allow businesses to bid / tender for work via an online auction that would help us as buyers procure at the most cost-effective price and allow businesses to bid against each other. So, putting tenders out to promote and get our clients to input everything onto an online auction and bid against each other. When I came to be a recruiter, one of my clients, a significant main contractor, was looking to put their suppliers through e-Auctions but didn't know where to start. It came up in conversation, so I volunteered the fact that I could come in and spend some time with their Board of Directors to talk them through an e-auction. How an e-Auction works, the type of software, and how you're going to manage your clients so the end-users knew how to bid successfully. It was an added value. Not many other recruiters out there could sit with their clients and talk to them about managing such a new process. There was no immediate monetary value for me, but I got to sit in front of the Board of Directors and decision makers at one time, hugely increasing my visibility & value. Not only was I able to talk them through how to run an e-Auction, but I could also talk to them about their recruitment needs whilst I had a captive 'client' audience.

What I say is an honest reflection of the answers you need. For example, I was working with a leading corporate construction contractor, and their recruitment process was overly protracted. It had a psychometric test, a first interview, a second interview, a third interview, then a 20-minute meet and greet with the MD. It was taking four to five months to find a successful placement.

They began asking me, "why are our offers being turned down? Why are we missing out on the best candidates?"

I told them "it's because your recruitment process is too long!" I was able to go and sit with them and suggest the following "do your PPA or your psychometric tests at the first interview stage, do the test in the office, interview them afterwards as a little introduction interview, get them back in for a technical second interview. And if they're good, make sure the MDs in the office on the same day and get them to pop in at the end of the 2nd meeting. You've done all you need to do across two interviews and in a much quicker timescale." This is offering a consultative service back to the client, "this is what the market is saying, and this is what I see as a consultant as to what is going wrong and how you can improve to get the best candidates." This approach means that I can add value and differentiate who I am against the rest of the market.

In the current Recruitment Mastery Group we have one member who has worked in internal recruitment for over ten years and decided to 'turn to the dark-side' and become a recruiter at the back end of 2020. I said to them, "you have ten years of internal recruitment experience, which separates you from the rest of the market. Normally recruiters go from being a recruiter to working internal and not the other way around – this differentiates you." It also adds vast amounts of value because this person will know how internal recruitment teams fail, what problems occur and what stopped them from getting the best people.

I look at internal recruitment consultants and see them as gatekeepers. And quite often, they will block the process. This particular member has seen it from the other side, so consultatively, they can and will add huge value to the recruitment process.

My purchasing background means that I can differentiate when I'm talking to Buyers because I am a qualified Buyer. I understand the supply chain, negotiation, frameworks, contracts, and how to work as a construction Buyer. It sets me apart from any of my competition.

Differentiating could be as little as doing a salary survey or adding value back to your market that your competitors don't. It could be that you're a specialist in the areas that you're recruiting, where you already have the insider dealing information or the market knowledge. That adds enormous amounts of value in regards to personal branding and social media.

Differentiation is great, but from a personal branding perspective, if you're not telling anyone about it, the only person who benefits is the person you're in conversation with. So that's why updating your network often is imperative. Take those examples and use them in your social media posts or your personal branding positioning and strategy.

Be ahead of the curve

Consistently shouting about what you do and how you do it differentiates you from your typical average recruiter who simply registers a job and sends a few CVs. You must be willing to have conversations even when there's not a definite requirement but be able spot the opportunity to be able to deliver. You must approach your relationships from different angles and be proactive. I know my market well enough to add value by putting candidates in front of clients they might not have considered as suitable or available. I don't know all the answers, and I certainly don't sit here and think that I know the conversations that clients are having behind closed doors, because I certainly don't. Recruiters are only generally informed after board meeting conversations and there is a confirmed requirement. Of course, I want those opportunities, but I also want to differentiate so that when I see good people, or I've worked with them before, I want to be able to go back to a client and say, "trust me, you want to see this person. They've become available, and they're worth taking the time to have a chat with."

I can see the added value of putting these people together, which differentiates me from your average recruiter. It differentiates me in a market where most people work 'day to day' in the same way and don't necessarily think outside of the box.

Differentiation is a mindset shift

You must think of a hurdle as an opportunity; if you see a hurdle as a stumbling block, you will only ever see stumbling blocks in front of you. What you want to see are opportunities. Otherwise, you will never go out of your way to do something because all you will see are the problems that lie ahead. If you sit there and think everything's an opportunity, it's always worth exploring. If somebody contacts me and advises they want to have a chat about something, or would I be interested in coming onto their podcast, or would I do a Q&A session with their team? I usually say YES and think about the consequences afterwards.

I could quite quickly shut down and say, no, I don't have the time. I'm too busy – maybe another time, but generally, I always accept because I don't know what value it will bring until the opportunity has been explored. Remember that there is an opportunity for an open conversation and understand that you don't know all the answers. Having a conversation with someone new could bring about an opportunity to further enhance you as a person. I think keeping an open mind, keeping an opportunistic outlook will lead you down a hugely positive and rewarding path either way.

Have a considered thought process, and don't be one dimensional. In fundamental terms, if you called me and said, "Steve, I need a Senior Estimator with a traditional, principally trained background." I know the market doesn't offer it, and those people aren't out there, but I know I can find a more junior person at a lower salary or a more senior person but closer to retirement. If I'm one dimensional, I'll take the job spec, I'll advertise it, I'll hope for some CVs, and maybe I'll get lucky and find one. You put the phone down, finish your coffee; that's the end of the conversation. The opportunity there is to go back to the client and advise what the market actually offers, not what their expectations are. Not being one dimensional is looking where the opportunity is to do something outside of the original brief.

Differentiation is always willing to think outside of the box and not to assume that you know everything. The assumption of absolute knowledge is the death knell. It's an oldie, but a goody – 'to assume makes an ass out of you and me!'

CHAPTER TWELVE

The Haters

(If this is relevant to you already, you've made it kid!)

'Haters' is one of my new favourite subjects. I am not a silent warrior looking for a conflict, but observing haters is akin to viewing bullies in the playground. As a child, I inherently stood up against bullies, and as an adult, I've found that the behaviour of bullies is much more complex and profound than you might think. I want to show that if you are authentically 'you' and receive 'hate', then you are probably doing something right.

Ironically, the more you do, the more people will object; it's all part of the natural progression. When you first start personal branding, social media posts, putting yourself out there, doing your first video or standing outside your comfort zone, the first flash of objection is probably the most difficult to take. You will often find that you've simply misinterpreted how somebody attempted to convey a written reply. In the beginning, you're already in a position where you're expecting someone to pull you down and thus, you can misread things. Somebody might suggest something that they think is constructive, and you can easily take offence to it. It might just be an honest difference of opinion. Once you get to the point where you are open to debate that's not personally vindictive, I think that's a positive thing. Having people disagree with you can be great, as it opens up some great conversation.

However, the last twelve months have given rise to a great deal more keyboard warriors. I think there are many more people online with fictitious accounts out there to cause upset and torment. I've noticed more of it, and I know these people are much braver behind a keyboard than in the flesh.

I've always believed that if people are writing derogatory comments that are personal or vengeful, I should treat them with kindness. I thank them for their comment. Once, I commented that the person was 'just in need of a big cuddle'. I don't respond that way usually, though – the easiest thing is to ignore them. You waste a lot of time otherwise. Even if I disagree with what someone has written, yet it's written well, I usually appreciate it regardless.

I don't think it's right to delete comments that you disagree with or are derogatory; after all, they're embarrassing themselves more than they are you.

Do I get haters? Yes. Since my first book's popularity, I now receive a fair amount of negative comments that I had never had before, but it depends on how you term 'a hater'. People have the freedom to express their opinion, but some are explicitly trying to pull you down. However, as they say, if you're getting haters, then you're doing something right!

The majority of people hating on you and pulling you down probably wish that they were in your shoes, doing what you're doing. Usually, you're doing something that they can't, or perhaps don't have the guts to do.

If you're getting haters, it means that people are paying attention to you which is a good thing, in my opinion.

If you're embarking on a personal brand journey and putting yourself out there, creating social media posts, you will get people who will hate you. People will comment. People will discuss your clothes, how you speak, the terminology you used, and they will critique what you've done. They will question you to try and trip you up and knock you down. They will try and attack your credibility. I'm not saying that it happens a lot, but it does happen from time to time. The more you progress on the journey, the more people will aim and see what they can do. The human race can be very unkind, and sometimes the bigger you are, the larger the target you are for people with insecurity issues.

You can see all around you; there's lots of debate around hugely important issues; like race and gender, that creates mass hysteria. It's always been that way, and maybe always will. It is our human nature that people will always be happy to offer an opinion, whether they are educated on the subject or not. We must remember that we don't get to control it.

On a smaller scale, as you progress on your personal branding journey, we can be offended by those opinions. Remember, though, the bigger you are, the public will express more opinions.

I've had people call me anonymously and say, "Is that Top Biller?" and then hang up – it's odd, but you've got to laugh. People can be weird, strange, random and delightful at times but I rest on the fact they I don't have any control over it. I go into each day humble and enjoying what I do. I'm hardworking, and I view it as all part of the journey. I don't know all the answers, and I make mistakes; therefore, I'm pretty happy for people to offer their opinions and thoughts. I do take things on board – positive criticism is excellent. I don't give any time to people attacking me, though. I draw the line there, and I ignore those people. I don't give them the time of day, they are probably miserable, and their comments are simply a projection of that unhappiness and insecurity.

A large part of the negative comments I receive come from the fact I wrote a popular book called 'Top Biller'. The recruitment world is full of big personalities, big egos, and competitive high-achievers. I'm not going to sit here and say I'm the most significant billing consultant on the planet – far from it. I'm not; in fact, I've worked with, managed and competed against far bigger billers, and I'm very comfortable with that. I didn't write Top Biller to say, "I am the biggest biller – look at what I'm doing, look what I've achieved; you should all come over here and copy me." However, with the nature of the title, some recruiter's naturally think, "I've billed much more than you – so how can you class yourself as the top biller?" This is typical of the ego 'puff-out' chest type competition.

If I saw a book called Top Biller, my first thought would probably be to wonder what that person billed. How does that person call themselves the top biller? What's the number or the value for that? And that's the problem; the market we're in is about high fives and the obligatory ego bump.

However, I didn't write the first book because I believe I'm the best out there and that no one can compete with me. The first book is about my journey, just as *this* book is. However, the book's title puts me in a position where haters can come flying at me to pull me down every day of the week because they think, that I believe, I know it all.

Top Biller was created to empower and motivate other recruiters. It was written with good intention, and I think that anybody that reads the book can glean that from the first few paragraphs.

Sometimes, I might spend a day or two running the hurtful comments through my head, and it can affect me. But I soon realise they are a tiny minority compared to the fantastic feedback and encouragement that I receive. As I write this, the Top Biller book has received 77%, five stars and 12%, four stars, and excellent reviews. It's funny how you can have so many five-star reviews, with reinforcing and reaffirming comments, and then you get that one negative comment, and it can completely throw you into a spin.

This is called negativity bias. It comes from when we were wilder and had to remember what things were dangerous and what we should avoid. Most of us, at least in the west, thankfully live in a predominantly safe world. Therefore, our negativity bias is a primitive yet very human part of our experience. It is self-preservation. If someone is speaking ill of you in the old days, they could seriously hurt you or your family, so our brains' negativity bias makes us cling to negative things that people say. We can learn to see past the negativity bias, but that's a whole other kettle of fish. I do propose you look it up, though.

Personal branding, social media marketing, and creating the ability to be the key person of influence means you must elevate yourself higher, which means that you're inevitably going to upset people. You're certainly going to ruffle people's feathers and push people into corners that they don't want to be in. If you're becoming the person that people want to talk to, it could be taking clients and business away from other people, so you're naturally going to upset people, even if your intentions are good. Even if you're doing everything ethically, honestly, and adequately, just simply by doing something better, you're going to disrupt the market. Some might appreciate the excellent competition and try to up their game and improve themselves. Some, however, will hate on you instead. That's because they're upset with the fact that you've gotten ahead of the game.

So, in summation, if you are beginning to get haters (and you're not doing anything to hurt others), it's most probably because your branding journey is growing in precisely the right direction. As Winston Churchill said, "You have enemies? Good. That means you've stood up for something, sometime in your life".

Sure, keyboard warriors and negative people aren't great, but they aren't worth your attention, so do your thing and get out there. It's going to happen anyway, so why not go through the process with your head held high.

I'm taking risks for my legacy to make sure that my kids have a great future and that the opportunities are there for them. I will stand in front of anything to protect my wife and my two boys. That is my WHY. Putting a post out there and having some random person write hateful comments is hardly on my priority radar and is certainly not going to deflect me away from the much bigger mission that I am on.

There are two kinds of people in this world:

- One type might experience something and think, "Oh, why did I have to go through that?" Those types then eagerly anticipate other people having to go through the same thing.
- The other type going through the same experience might think, "Oh, now I can help others who are going through this."

I want to be the latter.

I've made these mistakes, and I hope to help you avoid making the same blunders. I don't know all the answers, but I can talk through my journey and tell others what has worked for me. I appreciate that there are people behind where I am right now, and there are people in front of me. If you add value along the way, regardless of who your audience is, you will keep pushing forward. If you keep pushing outside your comfort zone and keep doing new things, sometimes you'll fall on your face, and sometimes it will work, and you sit there and think, "I'm delighted I did that". Everything I'm doing now, like the books, the podcasts, the recruitment training program, the strategy calls, the social media marketing, the personal branding, is all one massive journey, and what have I got to lose, but more importantly what have I got to gain?

There are no preconceived ideas of whether anything will be successful. I'm just going for it because that's where I am at this point. I do it with a humble outlook that hopefully has a good ending, and people get value from my journey along the way. If I get to a point where I stop adding value, then perhaps it's time to stop. But, at the moment, the network's growing and things seem to be going in the right way. Predominantly,

I'm enjoying the process. I like doing new things and putting myself out of my comfort zone. I think it's healthy.

If that means I tread on a few people on the way, and they throw stones at me, then I'll take it. Come at me! 😏 *You should do the same!*

Conclusion

Too many companies want their brands to reflect some idealized, perfected image of themselves. As a consequence, their brands acquire no texture, no character and no public trust.

— Richard Branson

Thank you for joining me on my personal brand journey. I hope that you have picked up many tips along the way.

As I always say, if I can go from being the successful, yet unassuming, procedure-led recruitment consultant to a global business influencer, then you can too! In this book, we looked at my journey across the following topics;

- **What makes you different?** – How to discover what makes you unique, and how to use that individuality to present to the world.

- **What is a personal brand and why is it important?** – How having a personal brand can hugely elevate your reputation and illuminate skillsets you might not have known

- **Writing a book** – How writing a book recognises you as an authority on the subject that you are writing about.

- **The power your personal brand holds** – How exploring being our authentic self and sharing all the trials and tribulations of our journey is a superpower.

- **Social media and the power of consistency** – How process and consistency in your social media posts will mean that you are continually on your audiences timeline.

- **How to grow your network** – How to grow a solid network, as without one there would be no point in trying to market anything at all! A good network is crucial to your success.

- **Adding value** – How continually giving back will grow your reputation and make you the go to person of expertise in your field.

- **Your network is your networth** – How you can utilise your network to increase your success.

- **Leverage** – How to utilise your network to open new doors.

- **Differentiating yourself** – How to put all of your new skills into action and start shaping the brand.

- **The haters** – How to recognise haters, and to realise that jealousy is one of the best forms of flattery.

A personal brand journey summary

My personal brand journey has been a rollercoaster with many ups and downs. There have been days when I lost sight of the end goal and other days when I've had laser focus. Above all else, I have learned that a solid personal brand journey is a persistent pursuit to show up and push forward consistently.

Before social media, it's important to remember how difficult it was to be noticed. We had to make every single contact with our audience via a phone call, email or post. In the present day, we can reach everyone in a single post and connect with individuals that would typically be out of reach. The ability to grow, interact and push a personal brand is at your fingertips, and you can make your audience and network come to you, allowing for warmer conversation than ever before. It's all waiting for you on a plate, but first, you must be willing to put yourself out there.

The current statistic is that only 1% of LinkedIn users engage and post content, which is crazy! What are the other 99% of users doing?

> ***"Observe the masses and do the opposite!"***
> (James Caan CBE, CEO Hamilton Bradshaw)

If 99% of users aren't posting and pushing a personal brand, which side will you be on? I would much rather be part of the 1% and be different to the crowd rather than standing aside and watching others progress.

My personal brand (at the time of writing) has allowed me to:

- Become the go to person for recruitment needs in my market (which leads to more placements and greater success!).

- Become the go to person for recruitment training, mentorship and coaching – globally!
- My personal brand has attracted my market to me, and now recruitment consultants want to work with me and for me.
- Clients and candidates want me to work with them as they feel like they already know me.
- Sold over 6,000 copies of 1st book – "Top Biller – The Life of a Recruiter" across 44 countries.
- Create Digital, Paperback and Audio copies to meet the demand.
- Launch my 2nd book.
- Grow an engaged social media network across all platforms.
  - https://www.linkedin.com/in/steveguest1/
  - https://www.instagram.com/steveguest/
  - https://www.facebook.com/steve.guest.520
- Build the global online 12 Week Recruitment Mastery Training programme.
- Establish a Recruitment Accountability Programme.
- Establish the Free Recruitment Mastery Facebook Group.
  - https://www.facebook.com/groups/recruitmentmasteryfree
- Become a recognised public event and keynote speaker.
- Be a guest on numerous podcast shows.
- Establish my podcast The Guestlist with Steve Guest.
- Establish The Guestlist with Steve Guest YouTube Channel.
- Conduct, host, and be a guest on LIVE chat shows across the globe.
- Conduct, host, and be a guest with businesses on live Q&A sessions.
- Receive constant requests to attend and speak at shows and events.
- Conduct oversubscribed webinars offering content and value to recruiters worldwide.
- Gain a captive, engaged and loyal network globally.

- Meet amazing people that are hugely motivational and inspiring.
- Connect, engage and grow.

Please connect with me via any of my social media channels for links to podcasts, YouTube channel, webinars, groups, socials and free resources.

Thank you for reading 'A Personal Brand Story', now it's time for me to give back to you. Please follow the link below for your free template of the "50 best LinkedIn posts" or email me directly:

http://bit.ly/Personalbrandstory or steve@sguest.co.uk

This free PDF offers everything you need to get started with your personal branding journey.

So all that remains is to ask – are you with me? Are you going to make it happen?

Get in contact; I would love to be a part of your personal brand journey. Why don't you put a social media post out of you holding this book, tag me in so I can get involved with the comments and I will send you an additional FREE gift.

Good Luck!

Lightning Source UK Ltd.
Milton Keynes UK
UKHW020638160821
388940UK00010B/688

9 781916 245921